PRAISE FOR *There I Wuz! A..*

"When we come across an aviator ... off the page. Eric Auxier is such an ...

—Karlene Petitt, Airline Pilot; CNN Correspondent; Author, *Flight to Success*

"With his signature brand of riveting prose, Captain Auxier brings aviation to life in vivid, spellbinding color."—Tawni Waters, Author, *Beauty of the Broken*

"Like watching a slide show of the life of a pilot. You will seriously enjoy this fast-paced read."—PaxView Jeff (paxview.wordpress.com)

"Great stories from the pointy end of the plane."

—Michael Lothrop, Pilot, Author, Stall Recovery (flymaine.blogspot.com)

"Eric takes our minds on a wild ride of fun, laughter, and hair-raising flying tales. A thriller in every sense of the term!"

—Jean Denis Marcellin, Pilot, Author, *The Pilot Factor*

PRAISE FOR *THE LAST BUSH PILOTS*

"TOP 100, BREAKTHROUGH NOVELS, 2013"—Amazon.com

"You won't want to put it down while the midnight sun still shines!"

—Airways Magazine

"Eric Auxier is the next Tom Clancy of aviation."—Tawni Waters, Author, *Beauty of the Broken*; *Siren Song*; *Top Travel Writers 2010*

"I flew through *The Last Bush Pilots* in one sitting, keeping my seatbelt securely fastened. A fast-paced tale, thoroughly enjoyed."

—John Wegg, Editor, *Airways* Magazine

"The author paints pictures with words that are every bit as beautiful and moving as anything ever drawn or photographed."—Aviationguy.com

"A page-turning adventure novel, where surviving is only half the battle."

—Mark L. Berry, Airline Pilot, Author, *13,760 Feet*

"As an Alaskan bush pilot, reading *The Last Bush Pilots* was like a glance in a mirror."—CloudDancer, Airline Pilot, Author, *CloudDancer's Alaskan Chronicles*.

PRAISE FOR CODE NAME: DODGER *Young Adult Spy/Fly Thriller Series*

WINNER—Remington Literary's Search for a Best First YA Novel

"An all-time fun ride! The author hit a big win on this. Looking forward to the series!"—Karlene Petitt, *Flight for Safety; Flight for Control; Flight to Success*

"Like *Harry Potter*, this YA novel is fun for kids of all ages."—Tawni Waters, Author, *Beauty of the Broken; Siren Song; Top Travel Writers of 2010*

"I'm 50 years older than the target market for this book, and I couldn't put it down!"—George Nolly, Airline Pilot, Author, *Hamfist* trilogy

Mission 2: Cartel Kidnapping: " I didn't think it was possible to improve on the first book, but it happened!"—Octavious L., Florida

Books and Novels by Eric Auxier

The Last Bush Pilots (*Amazon Top 100 New Novel Award, 2013*)
There I Wuz! Adventures From 3 Decades in the Sky—Volume I
Code Name: Dodger
    A Young Adult Spy/Fly Thriller Series for Kids of All Ages
        Mission 1: Operation Rubber Soul
        Mission 2: Cartel Kidnapping
        Mission 3: Jihadi Hijacking *(Release date November 2015)*

Also by Eric Auxier

Blog: Adventures of Cap'n Aux (capnaux.com)
Columnist—Airways Magazine, AirwaysNews.com
Regular Contributor—NYCAviation.com

Got eBook?

*If you purchased this book in print via Amazon, get the eBook version for only
$1.99! Color photos! Videos! Hotlinks and more!*

Link: amazon.com/author/ericauxier

*A portion of all author proceeds benefit the orphan charities
warmblankets.org and flyingkites.org*

THERE I WUZ!

ADVENTURES FROM 3 DECADES IN THE SKY
VOLUME II

BY ERIC "CAP'N AUX" AUXIER

Published by EALiterary Press.

Printed in the United States of America.

ISBN-13: 978-1512102819
ISBN-10: 1512102814

THERE I WUZ!

ADVENTURES FROM 3 DECADES IN THE SKY
VOLUME II

TABLE OF CONTENTS

DEDICATION

Dedicated to Allen, Patty and Gary.

Despite being my siblings, you're all still pretty much awesome.

FOREWORD by Mark L. Berry

MD-80 Captain, Author, Blogger, Audiobook Creator

The procedures commercial pilots follow are often written with the blood of our predecessors, mentors, and peers.

Even with thousands of hours logged in numerous aircraft types, we as commercial pilots learn something new every time we fly. In fact, that's a primary goal of professional pilots everywhere—continue to learn and evolve. We never know when some tidbit of information is going to become useful in an emergency or abnormal situation—so we study manuals, fly simulators, and attend annual recurrent training. But the best lessons happen unexpectedly.

Because the price for failure in an airplane is so high, that's what we do—we strive to learn from our own mistakes, and those who have flown before us. Sometimes pilot error is tragic, and other times we escape with only our egos damaged. Those tales that tarnish our self-perception while polishing our humility are the ones that potentially grow into legends.

And here's a collection of just those sort of stories that make even hardened aviators crack a smile and admit we are human.

Author and Captain Eric Auxier is not just a pilot, he is a true aviation advocate. He not only flies for his own satisfaction, he is dedicated to making our seemingly secret society—that's hidden behind bulletproof cockpit doors—less of a mystery to aviation enthusiasts.

I hope you will enjoy these insights into a world where excellence is revered, but we acknowledge that perfection can never be obtained.

Cheers,
Mark L. Berry

Mark's an airline pilot with an MFA from Fairfield University, author of a memoir 13,760 Feet—My Personal Hole in the Sky *(with 41 companion songs) and two novels* Pushing Leaves Towards the Sun *and* Street Justice, *contributing editor for* Airways *magazine, and former managing editor for* Mason's Road *literary journal.*

His work has also appeared in 4'33", Aerospace Testing Int'l, AOPA Flight Training, BMW Owners News, Connecticut newspapers, Epiphany, ERAU EaglesNEST, Graze, LIFT, MilSpeak Memo, Now What? The Creative Writer's Guide to Success, After the MFA, Port Cities Review, Rogue, So...Stories of Life, The Stoneslide Corrective, The Story Shack, TARPA Topics, Under the Sun, *and* Write This.

Now on Audible.com

13,760 Feet

MARK L. BERRY

A full-production, 15-hour audiobook, infused with 41 original songs

His memoir was recently released as a full-length audiobook on Audible.com

PREFACE—Welcome Aboard!

Ladies and gentlemen, from the Flight Deck, this is Cap'n Aux speaking. Welcome aboard Volume II of *There I Wuz!*

I hope you enjoyed Volume I, but if you haven't caught it, don't worry. Each book in this series stands alone—as does each story in this book—with its own tales of aviation adventure, humor, heartache and fun. Feel free to read them in any order you like.

Many of the stories you read here have appeared in one form or another on my *Adventures of Cap'n Aux* blog (capnaux.com), or in various magazines such as *Airways* Magazine, AirwaysNews.com, *Plane & Pilot*, *AOPA Pilot*, NYCAviation.com and the like. But never before have they appeared together in an anthology.

Moreover, inside you will find guest posts from other noted pilot-authors, such as international A330 pilot and CNN correspondent

Karlene Petitt, Gulfstream pilot and aerobatic champion Ron Rapp, as well as CRM expert, Lear 45 pilot and all-around fun guy, Jean Denis Marcellin.

One writer I am particularly honored to have aboard Volume II is Tawni Waters, author of the award-winning bestseller, *Beauty of the Broken*, which continues to garner awards, accolades and praises—including one of the world's most prestigious literary prizes, the International Literacy Association Award for Young Adult Literature.

While not a pilot, Ms. Waters writes—quite hysterically—about the time she navigated Mexico using only her . . . breasts. OK, 'nuff said—you just gotta read it! *Note to concerned parents: all stories in this book series are rated no worse than a very mild PG.*

I have also listened to your feedback from Volume I, calling for more, and longer, tales. In addition, you'll also find stories behind the stories, and as many photos as I can cram in. Except where otherwise noted, every story in this work is true, and represents what is, for me, a literal lifetime of adventures in the sky.

Whether you are a seasoned warrior of the sky, fledgeling pilot about to embark on your own lifetime of adventures, or a "chairborne" avgeek, I invite you to sit back, relax (well, as best you can, some of these stories are pretty hairy) and enjoy the ride!

Happy Adventures!

Eric Auxier, April 23, 2015

SECTION 1: Inflight Emergency

You're the Captain: Medical Emergency!

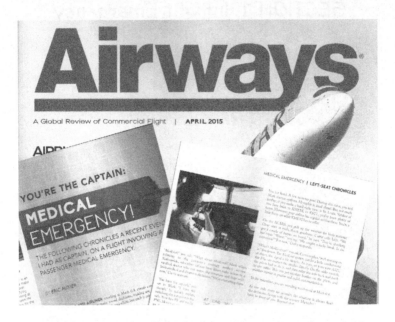

Originally published by Airways Magazine, April 2015
(An earlier version also appeared on NYCAviation.com in 2014)

"Captain, we've got a passenger losing consciousness."

The following article chronicles a recent event I had as Captain, on a flight involving a passenger medical emergency.

In an A321 airliner traveling Mach .8, events come at you at ten miles a minute. As Captain, you must make sound decisions, using imperfect information and limited time. Nearly every decision is not black and white, but each is critical, has consequences.

Now, you are Captain. You get to call the shots, feel the urgency, the burden of command. And you must make the right decisions that result in a safe, successful outcome.

"Ladies and gentlemen, this is your Captain speaking," you begin, briefing the passengers over the ships' PA during the final stages of boarding. "Welcome aboard Flight 312. We'll be cruising at an initial altitude of 32,000' . . ."

You expect Flight 312 to be routine. Pack 184 passengers—3 shy of capacity—into your Airbus A321, and ship off from KCLT (Charlotte, NC) to KPHX (Phoenix, AZ). Three hours and forty-four minutes of smooth sailing.

On this leg, you act as both PIC (Pilot in Command—i.e., Captain) and PF (Pilot Flying); your FO (First Officer) is PM, or Pilot Monitoring.

In other words, as PF, your sole job is to fly the plane.

As PM, your FO manages the flight—that is, handles all radio calls and communication, updates the weather, and generally deals with whatever comes up.

Today, that task falls upon the broad and capable shoulders of First Officer "Big Yo" Yohan.

True to form, takeoff and climb out go without a hitch.

But, as an airline pilot, you've got to be ready for anything. And today, that "anything"—as is often the case—begins with the *Ding!* of the call button from the lead flight attendant.

"Dominos Pizza," Big Yo answers in typical, smart-aleck FO-ese.

"Uh, put the pizza order on hold, boss," your First Flight Attendant Curtis says. "We've got a passenger back here that's losing consciousness."

You perk up, and trade alarmed glances.

"Who's the patient?" Big Yo asks.

"Elderly female. We've got her on oxygen and are asking for any medical personnel on board."

Big Yo looks to you.

"MedLink?" you ask.

"What about MedLink?" Big Yo relays, referring to the company's contract medical service. Nationwide, subscriber airlines have direct radio access to a medical doctor, who can assess the situation and help with both medical and diversion decisions.

"We're contacting them now," Curtis answers.

"You have the aircraft," you say to Big Yo.

"I have the aircraft," he quickly replies, switching the autopilot to his side. Now he's PF and you're PM. Moreover, since this is an abnormal situation, Yo will also handle the radios while you manage the crisis.

"Curtis," you chime in, "this is the Captain. I want to emphasize that your primary duty is to keep us informed. You are our eyes and ears back there. Let the other three flight attendants handle the emergency while you communicate with us as necessary."

"Aye aye, Cap'n," Curtis says.

You hang up.

"Whatcha wanna do, Boss?" Yo asks.

"Steady as she goes," you say. "Don't declare a medical emergency just yet. But let ATC know what's going on."

No major decisions until your Dispatcher Barry is in the loop, and you know more about the passenger's condition. And, more importantly, what the MedLink doctor says.

To inform the company, you use the MCDU (Multifunction Control Display Unit—the Airbus's computer) to type your situation into the ACARS (Aircraft Communications Addressing and Reporting System—lots of acronyms in the aviation biz, and especially the Airbus.)

You hit Send.

A few minutes pass. During this time, you and Yohan discuss options.

Memphis is dead ahead. But not much farther, if you make a hard right turn, is St. Louis. Neither of you have been to KMEM; to KSTL, you've been plenty of times. Moreover, your airline has regular service there. You're a little fuzzy on what KMEM has to offer.

On the ACARS, you pull up the weather for both stations. Clear skies at both, thank goodness.

Curtis calls back. "We got a couple of nurses on board," he says. "They're checking her vitals."

"Great," you say. "We caught a lucky break. Is she conscious?"

"For now."

"What's MedLink say?"

"Still working on it."

You frown. The MedLink system can be a little cumbersome at times, the signal a bit sketchy. At least on your new A321, the FA's can contact them directly. On the older models, the pilots had to do it, and then relay the info back and forth to the cabin. Yet another burden on the pilots, and another barrier to precise and quick communication.

In the meantime, you are traveling westbound at Mach .8. At one mile every six seconds, the situation is always fluid; the decisions change with the scenery. KMEM is now a half hour in front of you. Beyond that, you note, is KLIT (Little Rock), and KMCI (Kansas City.)

Dispatcher Barry comes back via the ACARS. He informs you the company has a good station at KMEM; no need to add extra time on the flight with a diversion to KSTL.

After discussing it with Yohan, you all agree on KMEM. But if you're going to land, you need to start down soon. Very soon.

Curtis calls back. "She's out again," he informs you. "MedLink advises us to divert."

"Roger that."

You nod to Yo.

The trigger has just been pulled.

Suddenly, everyone's very busy.

As Yo declares a medical emergency on ATC and requests vectors straight to Memphis, you brief Curtis. "OK, you've got twenty-five minutes before you're on the ground," you say, as you type the new destination in the MCDU. "I'll make a PA to the passengers as soon as I get the chance."

As Yo turns direct for Memphis and begins his high dive, you type KMEM as the new destination into the MCDU, then update the weather. Good skies. No need for a time-consuming ILS approach.

"Light winds, Yohan," you advise. "Which runway you want?"

You study your airport charts.

"Since we're approaching from the east," he replies, "let's do a straight-in to 27."

"Sounds good," you say, typing it in.

Loaded to the gills with fuel and passengers, you could be close to an overweight landing. You do a quick mental calc on the landing weight: approximately 178,000 pounds.

Yep, overweight.

That gives you two options: Land overweight, or spin circles to burn off fuel. Another fuzzy decision to make. Risk an overweight landing to help a possibly critical patient, or burn precious time and risk losing her?

You call the back. "Any updates, Curtis?"

"That's a negative, Cap. She's still out, and we lost the MedLink connection again."

"Damn," you mumble. You take a deep breath. "OK, Curtis. Touchdown in 20 minutes."

With her medical condition unknown—and possibly dire—and with MedLink unable to advise, you decide the heavy landing is worth the risk.

A quick call to KMEM station on the Number 2 radio. They're ready for you, gate C-8.

You pull out the QRH (Quick Reference Handbook), and turn to the Overweight Landing checklist. With Yo still bombing into KMEM at 330+ knots, you run the checklist solo, reviewing procedures, considerations and calculations.

One major issue: you may be too heavy for a go-around (aborted landing). You flip to the chart and calculate. You breathe a sigh of relief. Overweight, but still light enough for a go-around. Next, you flip to another set of tables and calculate landing distance. You eyeball the airport diagram again.

"Hey, Yohan," you say. "I'm gonna overrule you on Runway 27. Tell them we want 36 Center. It's 2,000 feet longer and is also closer to our gate."

"Roger that," he replies, accepting your decision in an instant. He keys the mike. "Memphis approach, Flight 312. We're gonna need 36 Center."

Since you are a Medical Emergency aircraft, ATC gives you priority, no questions asked. In short, you get what you want.

"Flight 312, turn left heading 200°, vectors dogleg base for 36 Center."

Yo reads back the clearance and turns to 200°, as you type the runway change into the MCDU and set up the ILS. While the weather is severe clear, the ILS will help Yo stay on the proper track and glideslope. Especially with an unfamiliar airport.

As you bomb through 10,000 feet, Yo throws out full speed brakes to maintain 250 knots, the speed limit below 10. As an emergency aircraft, you could wave that speed restriction, but you'd have a lot of 'splainin' to do afterwards. Besides, an overweight jet takes oodles of time to slow down. Oodles and oodles of time.

"Flaps one," Yo commands.

"Flaps one," you reply, pulling the flap lever back to the first notch.

The amber too slow bar, hovering near your speed, begins to recede. At this weight, you are between a rock and a hard place: barely five knots between max Flap speed and minimum flying speed. Moreover, the heavy, clean jet wants to go fast. Simply put, you can't just "go down and slow down."

Knot by precious knot, the airplane, ever so reluctantly, slows.

"Hey, Yohan," you say. "I know you're busy, but I need your attention for the last part of the Overweight Landing checklist."

Yo takes a deep breath. "Go ahead, Boss."

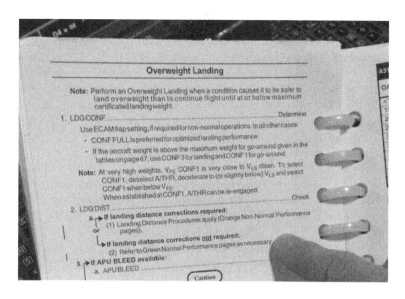

You read the final notes to him. "'At touchdown, land as smoothly as possible'—*Duh!*" you add. You chuckle with Yo, the humor helping to break the tension. "I'll record the vertical speed from the VSI. 'On touchdown, use max reverse thrust and apply brakes as necessary'"—

"Flaps two," Yo interrupts.

"Flaps two," you reply. As PF, Yo gets to interrupt you at any time to fly the plane. Again, as always, Priority One is FLY THE PLANE.

You continue. "'Make an overweight landing entry in the logbook. A maintenance inspection may be required before next flight.' Overweight Landing Checklist—Complete."

"Roger that."

Since you are unfamiliar with the airport, and Yo has his hands full flying and talking on the radio—not to mention slowing down the overweight juggernaut—you brief the approach for him.

"I have Memphis page 11-7, ILS Runway 36 Center approach." You read off the revision date.

Yohan glances at his chart, "I agree, ILS 36 Center, 11-7. Same revision date."

"Highest MSA is 2,500 to the East, off of MEM VOR. ILS frequency 110.5, ITSE, tuned and identified, inbound course 360 degrees . . ."

"Flight 312, turn right heading 330," ATC cuts in, "cleared ILS 36 Center, contact Memphis Tower on one one niner point seven."

Yo replies and contacts tower, who clears you to land. You finish the brief. One last thing for you to do. You pick up the PA.

"Ladies and gentlemen," You begin, "this is your Captain speaking. As you are probably aware, we have a medical issue on board and are diverting to land in Memphis. We will be touching down in five minutes. We will need everyone's cooperation today by remaining in your seats when we arrive at the gate—"

"Gear down, Flaps 3, Landing Checklist."

"Gear down, Flaps 3," You repeat, do so, then continue on the PA, "—to allow emergency medical personnel onboard. We are hoping to continue on our way to Phoenix within the hour. Thank you for your cooperation."

You hang up and read the Landing Checklist. "Engine mode Norm, Landing gear, verify, Down, Three Green."

"Down three green," Yo repeats, then adds, "Flaps Full."

"Flaps Full. Landing Checklist complete. Cleared to land 36 Center."

On short final, to break the tension one last time, you say the famous Leslie Nielson line from the movie, *Airplane!*, still quoted to this day in cockpits worldwide.

"I just want you to know: we're all counting on you."

The gambit works. Yo chuckles, then pulls off one of the smoothest greaser landings in the history of landings. So gentle, in fact, that a maintenance check *won't* be required. You don't know whether to be proud or jealous. Hell, you're both.

At the gate, you once again jump on the PA. "This is the Captain. Remain seated."

Paramedics board the plane and tend to the passenger. They half-carry her off, now awake but still quite dazed. Her daughter deplanes with her.

You nod to Yo, who turns off the seatbelt sign.

"Ladies and gentlemen, this is your Captain speaking," you announce, "I want to thank you for your cooperation. We will be refueling and departing as soon as possible to Phoenix. For now, feel free to stretch your legs, but please remain on board to help expedite our departure."

Sure enough, KMEM is a crack station. Despite the baffling arrival of different metal (your A321 was the first they'd ever seen, as opposed to the E190's they are used to servicing), you are closed and on your way in record time. You arrive in KPHX not one hour late, if two passengers light.

As Captain, you will have to fill out the requisite paperwork within 48 hours. Otherwise, for you, the case is closed. But first, you want to conduct a Post-flight debrief with the crew.

As you gather the crew in First Class to discuss the event, you start by saying, "I thought you all did an outstanding job in back today, and that will be reflected in my report. I especially want to commend you, Curtis, who kept your cool throughout, and kept us well-informed." They nod their gratitude. You run them through a quick summary of the event, emphasizing several important points. You finish by asking, "Does anyone have any comments, criticisms or questions about what we did right, or what we could have done better?"

The discussion continues for another 15 minutes, all of you learning a little more about CRM (Crew Resource Management), crew communications, and emergencies. While you are proud of the crew's near-flawless execution, next time, each one of you will perform that much better.

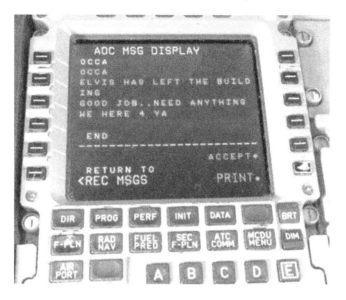

Congratulations on a safe and successful outcome, Captain!

Medical Emergency: Post Flight Debrief

In an airplane, nothing beats experience. That's why it's so critical for airline pilots to have thousand of hours in the cockpit. For example, I learned to make this exact initial briefing to Curtis—that is, emphasize that his primary duty was to keep us informed. Otherwise, "our eyes and ears in back" may go deaf and blind . . . which happened to me during another medical emergency.

Our lead flight attendant said to us, "She's not going to make it," and hung up. Repeated calls to the cabin went unanswered.

With visions of all flight attendants busy defibrillating a heart attack victim, we high dived into Kansas City. On the ground and in the gate, the flight attendant said, "Oh, I only meant she was in the bathroom throwing up and didn't want to continue."

Again, communication—especially during an emergency—is critical.

This is a good lesson in CRM—Crew Resource Management. In the old days, the Captain was God, and everyone else obeyed. He made all the decisions, and everyone blindly followed. In today's enlightened environment, every crew member is valuable and respected. The Captain is still the decision maker, and has final authority. But s/he values and considers everyone's input.

At all times, one pilot was flying the plane, while the other was handling the emergency.

The moment we heard there was a possible medical emergency, I gave Yohan the PF duties. Moreover, in a "non-normal" situation such as this, whether a passenger issue or a mechanical one, the PF usually works the primary radio as well, talking with ATC, while the PM handles all aspects of the emergency. At our airline, normally it's the Captain who handles it. I agree with this philosophy. The FO's are plenty experienced and trained to fly the plane themselves, while talking with ATC and also keeping the Captain in the loop as to what's going on.

As you can see from the narrative, in a "non-normal" situation, things are happening, and fast. Split-second decisions have to be made, all the while with ever-changing conditions, distractions and interruptions. For example, ATC can call at any time, even in the middle of a checklist.

In this narrative, I've tried to convey the urgency of the situation. The PIC has to balance the severity of the emergency with the reality of flight conditions; i.e., what is safest? The entire flight must not be jeopardized for the sake of one passenger; even so, the passenger's medical issue is paramount.

Real decisions, in real time, have to be made.

Finally, while time is critical, the PIC must resist the temptation to create a self-induced time constraint. That is, increase pressure on the crew with an unrealistic desire to get on the ground. Short of an inflight fire, any "non-normal" can be met—properly, and in its time.

Karlene Petitt: A330 Versus the Thunderstorm

Pilot—Author—Blogger

"Stall! Stall! Stall! the plane cried."

International airline pilot, author and CNN consultant Karlene Petitt is also one of our fellow *Formation Bloggers*. Each month, our team of eight pilot-bloggers join forces to discuss an important aviation topic.

Mother of three and grandma of six, Karlene is quick-witted, sassy, and a hopeless overachiever who is currently working on her PhD at Embry Riddle and writing yet another aviation thriller—all the while traipsing the globe in her A330.

In this scene from her second novel, *Flight For Safety*, beloved character Darby—a quick-witted, sassy A330 pilot (now, where did Karlene come up with that one?)—faces a, shall we say, *tense moment* in her Airbus.

Sadly, Karlene still has yet to give me Darby's phone number.

(Note to Parents: mild PG language, including the sh*t word.)

Darby Bradshaw—every younger man's dream and older man's regret.

While Darby is a character in my novels, she is also one of the most loved female pilots, by men and women alike. You can follow her on Twitter at @DarbyFlys. Whether she is attempting to lighten the mood with a strip tease, drinking wine in the hot tub with another bad choice in men, or flying an approach to minimums, readers can't help but to fall in love her.

Many people ask, "Who is the real Darby?" I would have to say she's a little bit of all female pilots living in a man's world of aviation, doing and saying what we all wish we could.

While Darby can fly a plane better than most, says what is on her mind, and deals head-on with anything that comes her way, she has the strength to stand her ground no matter what. Until she's in a plane, where diplomacy must always prevail.

Have you ever experienced a moment with another crewmember, a chief pilot or a situation that you kept your mouth shut and later thought of all the things you wished you would have said? Well, Darby says them. Thus female pilots everywhere can live vicariously through Darby's life, wishing we all had her confidence, strength, and attitude.

Why do the male readers love her? Well, I suspect they just want to sleep with her. But that is a story for another chapter. Warning to all—don't try to kill her, especially in a plane. Which is what happens on this particular flight between Narita and Singapore…

Four hours into their flight to Singapore, turbulence bounced their aircraft wildly. Storms were blooming ahead, but it was Keith who worried Darby, not the weather.

"Are you okay, Captain?" she asked.

"I'm fine," he said, wiping beads of sweat from his forehead.

He didn't look fine. He had lost most of his suntan within the last few minutes and looked like her alabaster sheets, turning whiter with each mile. The fact that those miles were passing at .82 Mach left her wondering at what point he would become a ghost.

"What's the max turbulent penetration speed?" he asked.

"Do you seriously not know?" Darby said. He had given her an aural in the briefing room, and enough was enough. He wasn't even a check airman. The night was way too long, she was tired, and had enough of his arrogance.

"I know what it is. I want to know if you know."

"You need to stop with the questions already," Darby spat. "This flight is exhausting enough as it is. If you don't pay attention to what you're doing you're going to kill us all, and that will really piss me off!"

"Okay, dammit. I forget what it is between the different models, but I think we should be flying it."

"No kidding!" She set .78 Mach, despite it being his leg. Backlit clouds flashed beyond the glareshield and crept closer, narrowing their window of opportunity to sneak through the storm.

"I think we should turn to the right and fly around that cell," Darby said.

"Left is a shorter distance. We'll get through this shit quicker."

"Look at the winds. Flying downwind of that cell will eat us for lunch."

"We'll be fine," Keith said spinning the heading bug.

The A330 barreled forward un-intimidated by the pounding it was taking. Darby reached forward and adjusted the scale on the map to display the ten-mile range, creating a clearer picture of the weather in relation to their path. She watched the next waypoint on her electronic map approach, and picked up the clipboard to confirm they were on course. The storm grew on all sides of them in equal proportion to her discomfort. She jolted with the plane and grabbed the glareshield.

Clouds grew, rapidly surrounding their Airbus. This weather system was more expansive than forecasted. Cells were building higher and closer than she was comfortable with. Up and down Keith turned the radar knob. It was obvious he did not know how to use it. They had an automated system, which made life easier...or was supposed to.

"If you leave the switch in auto, it paints worse than it is. Avoid the red and you're safe." His fingers continued to work the radar. "You don't want to break that little thing off, do you?" she said.

"That's all I need tonight."

Lightning was on all sides of them. The turbulence was so bad she wished she had worn her sports bra. Another jolt and she looked up to the overhead panel. What the hell?

"The seatbelt sign's off," she said reaching up and flipping the switch on.

"That should have been on for the previous twenty minutes!"

"I thought it was."

"Give a PA," he snapped.

She picked up the handset, "Ladies and gentlemen remain seated with your seatbelts fastened, we'll be through this in no time."

Since Captain Overloaded did not think of it, she reached down and turned the ignition to On. Heavy rain was below them, but what was in front screamed warning. Darby's nerves pushed her closer to the edge with each bounce. She was furious allowing herself to be sucked into this trap. She should have been more assertive. They were in the middle of a friggin' storm, bouncing at the tops, with buildups going higher on all sides. Lightning flashed out all windows.

"*Boom*," a deafening bang rang out and shook the plane. Darby jumped. They had been hit by lightning and it sounded like a sledgehammer slamming the side of the aircraft. The visibility decreased in a flash as rain beat on their windshield. The noise was deafening and she could feel the thunder reverberate in her bones. The plane bounced wildly.

They broke out of the intense rain and a light show grander than she had ever seen flashed on all sides of their plane. They were stuck. The radar painted red across her map on her navigation display. She saw one little hole they could sneak through. Hopefully it would not close in on them, as this was their only option.

"We need to turn left." When he did not respond she pulled the heading knob and said, "Heading select," and turned the selector to 160 degrees—the best course to get through the crud. "There's a hole this way."

"Yeah. Thanks," he said. "I see that."

They were bouncing like maniacs. Her eyes darted in and out of the flight deck and down to the map. Darby's heart raced. She placed a hand on the glareshield and said, "Hold on Baby," and then reached up and turned off the flight deck lights to get a better picture outside.

Rain streamed up the windshield. *What the ...?* Rain was supposed to fall down, not up. At 450 knots forward motion…is this even possible? The outside air temperature was -50C and the total air temperature was -21C. Liquid water at these temps? Darby had never seen such a thing. She turned the flight deck lights back on, and then…

Beep. Beep. Beep. Ding. Ding. Ding. The master warning and master caution lights flashed and the airplane cried warning as both the autopilot and autothrust disconnected.

Their airspeed indications dropped to 80 knots.

"Stall! Stall! Stall!" the plane cried.

"We're not stalling," Darby yelled. "Look at our speed." She pressed the data button on the MCDU and then selected GPS data. "We've got a ground speed of 486 knots."

The flight directors had disappeared, and a roar like machine gun fire attacking the plane vibrated the flight deck. Messages displayed rapidly across the ECAM and were being replaced by others faster than she could see what they were.

"Holy shit!" Keith yelled. One hand grabbed the thrust and his other grabbed the stick.

"Don't do anything!" Darby yelled over the noise. "Let the plane fly."

Ding.

Darby's eyes flashed back to her PFD. Their pitch was supposed to be at 3 degrees for level flight. They were at 10 degrees and increasing.

"Stop climbing," Darby yelled. The A330 could pitch up from 10 to 12 degrees very rapidly without much effort and a new pilot helping that effort was a mixture for disaster.

"What?"

"Don't climb. Bring the pitch down to three degrees."

Ding.

"But I let go of the stick," Keith yelled. "It shouldn't be climbing."

"It's going where you told it to go," Darby shouted as she pushed the stick forward. "We have to put it on 3 degree line."

"DUAL INPUT!" a synthetic voice blared over the speakers. Keith was back on the controls—they were both flying the plane so she let go as he corrected the pitch. She focused on level flight and her hand hovered over the stick until she was sure they had the same goal.

Once level, she moved her hand to the glareshield to hold on, but kept a watchful eye on the pitch attitude.

Ding.

Unlike the Boeing, the A330 trimmed to relieve elevator pressure for whatever pitch attitude the pilot wanted without the pilot's help. It was some g-loading thing and beyond her pay-grade. But when Keith let go of the stick after pulling back, the stick moved to neutral but the nose stayed pointed up because Keith had put it there.

Ding.

This was the first plane Darby flew that the pilots did not trim. It took an effort to pull a Boeing into a stall with cruise power without touching the trim. Not the Airbus in Alternate Law. The A330 was smart, but not smart enough to outthink a pilot who was giving it bad commands when the plane was having technical difficulties. Darby kept a watchful eye on all parameters.

"What the hell's happening?" Keith said, breathing rapidly.

Ding.

"You're in Alternate Law. Just fly what you've got." But he had a death grip on the stick and worked it hard. "Just little pressures to keep her level. Quit jerking the stick like you're whacking off, just fly the plane."

Ding.

"What about our power?" Keith asked. "I think the autothrust is off." The plane bounced and rocked.

Ding.

"Don't rock the wings, you're inducing instability," she said. "Your autothrust is off. Don't worry." Her senses were so overloaded that the *ding* occurring every five seconds turned into background noise that her brain tuned out. By leaving the thrust levers alone, the power would remain in the last setting. If it were good enough before, it was good enough while they stabilized and one less thing to worry about.

Once he settled down and the rolling motion slowed Darby said, "We're in thrust lock. That's the *ding*. The plane's holding power for .78 Mach. We're good if you don't climb."

Ding.

Darby reached for the thrust levers. "I think we've had enough warnings for one night." She pulled the thrust out of the climb detent and set the power to 83% N1.

She checked the engine instruments and the MCDU and said, "We're at 83% N1. Our GPS speed is not decreasing. We're maintaining altitude. Just baby her at level flight."

Darby's hand was lightly around the stick with her thumb hovering over the 'take the plane' button, ready to kick him out and take control if he started a climb again. Pitching up at this altitude was a slippery slope she did not want to experience.

The turbulence was moderate to severe. The plane jolted and inadvertently Keith banked. Then his rolling action began again. Back and forth. Each time he rolled farther.

Not again. "I got it," she said. "Give me the stick." She was hoping he would just take his hand off and the plane would stop rolling, but that wish went unanswered.

"I'm fine," he said, but the banking grew worse and he pitched up again.

"The hell you're fine!" He was rolling left. Then right. Then left. 10 degrees one way and then 15 the other, and increasing. In Alternate Law they had no protections. She suspected they were in Alternate Two where the roll rate response was about double the normal rate. He could roll her over on her back. And he was climbing again.

Shit. Shit. Shit. Darby pressed the takeover button on her stick. She locked out his stick and took control of the plane. A red arrow illuminated in front of him and pointed her way as a loud synthetic voice broadcasted, "Priority right."

It was career suicide locking out a captain at Global, but at least she would live to do the rug dance. *I will not die in this plane tonight!* The thought of living made overriding the captain that much easier to swallow.

He fought the plane. Each time he moved his stick a green CAPT light illuminated in front of her, telling her to not let go of the takeover button. He did not have a clue that she had taken control. His actions were for nothing.

Darby's heart raced. Sweat dripped into her eye and she brushed it away with the back of her hand.

She pushed the nose down to a level attitude while rolling out of the bank. They were heading directly into the heart of the storm. She moved the stick left to fly between two areas of intensity and then rolled the wings level.

"I got it," she said. He was not aware of what she had done. "Keith!" she yelled. "I got the plane! I'm flying. Relax." He released his hand and committed to being a passenger.

Once stabilized on a good heading she released the stick to neutral and the plane stopped rolling. She kept a gentle hand on the stick. The A330 was a stable plane, always looking to find its center of balance.

Darby did what she could. The rest was up to the Airbus. The turbulence was only light to moderate. The clouds at their altitude and higher were behind them and moving the opposite direction. Their instruments were back.

She reached up and cycled the flight directors off and back on and then engaged Keith's autopilot. She pressed the autothrust button and then pushed the thrust levers back into the climb detent. Power was restored to the Airbus thrust management system.

Everything looked good—on the surface.

(Note: This was an excerpt from *Flight For Safety*, but *Flight For Control* is the first in the series.)

Karlene Petitt is an Airbus A330 pilot living in Seattle, with 28-years airline experience; type rated on the B727, B737, B757, B767, B747-200, B747-400 and A330 aircraft; 22-years instructing in simulators on Boeing aircraft, while flying the line; authored numerous airline flight training program; founder of Aviation Safety International; currently working on her PhD in  aviation with Embry Riddle Aeronautical University; and the author of the novels* Flight For Control, Flight For Safety, *and the motivation book,* Flight To Success, Be the Captain of Your Life.

SECTION 2: Lessons Learned (the Hard Way)

THE CASE OF THE MISSING NOTAM

Originally published as "Listen Up!" in Plane & Pilot Magazine August 1990

"I could almost do it in my sleep. Perhaps that was what I was doing."

This is the second article I ever sold to a magazine. As I mentioned in *There I Wuz! Volume I*, I quickly found out that the dumber your mistakes, the easier it was to sell a piece about it.

And this story sold easily.

First published in *Plane & Pilot* August 1990 issue, this story found new life on my *Adventures of Cap'n Aux* blog. Again, it became one of the more popular posts that year.

I had been flying for a Phoenix-based charter company for about three months, had a few years' flight instructing and 1300 hours in my logbook, and had already settled into the company's bread-and-butter run: the Grand Canyon tour. Now, as an experienced tour pilot—or Ditch Driver, as we called ourselves—I could almost do it in my sleep. . .

Perhaps that was what I was doing on this day.

The sun was just peeking through the office window shades when the Flight Service Specialist answered the phone. I absent-mindedly rattled off the flight plan, all the while crunching weight and balance numbers on a calculator. The weather brief was just that—brief—as I knew it would be: severe clear and not a cloud in the state. CAVU, as we called it, "Ceiling and visibility unlimited.

Another boringly perfect fall day in Arizona.

"All Navaids operational," the briefer continued, while I pondered a glitch in my weight and balance calculations, "NOTAM (Notices to Airman) out for 'temporary' landing runway three."

"Runway three," I muttered, "thanks. Once we're airborne, we'll call you on one twenty-two point six to activate." I hung up and finished calculating the final c.g. (center of gravity.)

On the way out to the plane, something in the back of my mind whispered, runway three...wonder why he bothered saying that. The tower doesn't even open for another hour....

The thought slipped away as Debra, our office manager, introduced my passengers, four tourists from Japan. I smiled and led them to our Cessna Centurion.

The hour-and-a-half flight up was smooth and uneventful. But as the Canyon neared, my workload increased dramatically.

Flying through the Canyon, the Ditch Driver switches into hyperdrive: fly the plane, narrate the tour, watch for Ditch traffic, radio checkpoints to others, and listen for other Ditch Drivers transmitting checkpoints.

"Cessna seven eight Victor, you are cleared to land . . ."

I had my hands full, but continued with confidence—no, overconfidence.

"On your right we have Confucius Temple," I sang into the intercom as we soared past that natural rock statue. I keyed the mike and announced crisply, "Canyon traffic, Centurion seven eight victor, Confucius, eight point five, westbound."

I punched the number two radio monitor button and a second voice spoke into my headphones, superimposed over the number one radio chatter:

"...Grand Canyon airport information Mike, time..."

"On your left," I continued, "is my favorite, the giant rock scorpion."

"...altimeter two niner niner seven, temporary landing runway three...."

". . . on TEMPORARY Runway 3."

I set the altimeter and announced, "Centurion seven eight victor, Scorpion Ridge, eight point five, inbound for the airport."

Again I had missed that single, subtle word, temporary.

As we sailed past the south rim, I flipped to Grand Canyon Airport Tower frequency.

"Canyon tower, Centurion seven eight victor, Cocopah Point, landing with Information Mike."

"Centurion seven eight victor, enter on a right base for three."

"Roger."

"Centurion seven eight victor," came the call on final as I was glancing around the cabin to check my passengers' seatbelts, "cleared to land, temporary runway three."

Turning back to the controls, I answered, "Cleared to land, roger."

On short final, I noticed something strange on the runway. An object of some kind. As we neared, the object grew to the shape of a man, two men, three men on the runway!

The Twin Otter behind me calmly asked over the radio, "Hey, isn't that guy lined up on the wrong runway?"

Suddenly, the word TEMPORARY flashed through my thick head.

"Seven eight victor, go around! Men and equipment on the runway!"

I was ramming the throttle in as the tower called, "Seven eight victor, go around! Go around, men and equipment on the runway!"

The workers, alerted by the sudden surge of power, scattered. As we aborted the landing and climbed back out, I frowned at my startled passengers, pointing to the workers on the runway as if it were their fault.

The Japanese watched in amazement the frenzied rout of escapees.

I continued around the pattern and landed—this time, on the parallel taxiway, the temporary runway 3. During the slow taxi to the ramp, I mentally cowered from the reproachful eyes of the controller, construction workers, and the other professional pilots who surely must have seen my blunder.

This story is now filed away in the *There I Wuz!* arsenal of cocktail party stories. But down inside, when I tell it with a wink and a smile to a captive (and, I make sure, nonflying) audience, deep down inside I know it was nothing to be laughed at. It is an embarrassing reminder of my own stupidity, when I almost let complacency get the upper hand.

Now, when I find myself tracing the same old route from point A to point B, I remember: always pay attention . . . .

For, if you write off a flight as just another routine, one day, your plane might write you off.

Case solved.

Jean Denis Marcellin: Fire in the Hull!

Commercial Pilot—CRM Expert—Author—Blogger

My captain's voice startles me: "We have a FIRE!"

When I first encountered JD Marcellin's blog at planesimplesolutions.com, I was so impressed that I immediately wrote a post for my own entitled, *My Favorite Bloggers*—with him as the headliner!

We pilots tend to see ourselves as Type A problem solvers, and have an innate disdain for all that "touchy-feely charm school stuff." Emotional sensitivity is for sissies—I'm Captain Kirk, dammit!

Enter Jean Denis Marcellin.

A commercial pilot, CRM (Crew Resource Management) and human factors safety expert, Mr. Marcellin is constantly dragging us back to reality. He greys up our black and white world by throwing our *Safe operation of an aircraft* mandate against the the Human Factor filter.

He challenges us to dig deep, go all introspective, and ask ourselves, Are we *really* flying this airplane in the safest possible manner—by taking the human condition into account?

What's more, in his book, *The Pilot Factor*, he uses awesome examples of said Human Factor that include such pop culture icons as Cap'n Kirk, Men in Black, and superheroes like The Avengers.

In short, he's my kinda writer!

It was another beautiful day of flying. Long, but fulfilling. Medevac operations tend to carry a certain *je ne sais quoi* when it comes to going the extra mile to make sure a patient gets the care they need in time. A drive that allows us to go through that 13th or 14th hour of duty day, knowing it was for a good cause. It makes us feel good; it drives us to push ourselves even more. After all, are we not a bit akin to angels—flying and saving lives? But despite our love for comparing ourselves to larger-than-life heroes or grand characters like Captain Kirk, every pilot—inside and out—is only but a humble human.

Human nature is fickle. One moment flying high, the next firmly grounded to pavement, pilots find themselves stuck in a dichotomy of worlds that often carry challenges, even to the most experienced. After a long day of over-12hr duty, Fatigue sets in despite the best of intentions or efforts to fight it. It settles in, stealthy, quietly opening the door to its sibling, Complacency.

Phoenix Vice! JD wings in from Canada in his Lear 45, and I whisk him away in the AuxMobile for a little well-earned pilot down time!

And so our story continues. With another long day coming to an end, we were finally heading home. Soon. Soon... First, however, we needed to land at one more destination to drop off a patient in dire need of medical assistance. We'd come in from hundreds of miles away, but that's why we did what we did. Remote areas of the country meant only airplanes could cover to the vast distances to the best-equipped hospitals. We were flying ICU's (Intensive Care Units), capable of delivering babies airborne or performing life-saving treatments to sustain patient lives while enroute to the doctors and equipment they needed.

Nearing our destination, the mood remained light despite the increasingly busy segments of approach and landing. The weather was truly gorgeous, and we were doing what we loved most—flying. Our airplane, a PC-12NG (Next Generation) was a remarkable work of art, science and a sprinkle of magic put together, giving us incredible capabilities and situational awareness through a top of the art computerized system. If anything would go wrong, the airplane would let us know. For now, though, all we had to do was enjoy the beautiful day, eventually landing that airplane just perfect while each wheel kissed the pavement gently.

The venerable PC12. Photo courtesy JD Marcellin.

But our work was not over. As soon as we cleared the active runway, ground control issued our next clearance, directing us towards our parking spot where we were to transfer the patient to the awaiting ambulance. Once I read back the clearance, my mind immediately went to the paperwork, while the captain diligently taxied around the airport. Stifling a yawn, I let my attention digress from the airplane itself, while my eyes wandered around the checklist quickly. Knowing we had to turn around quick to make it home on time, I then picked up the loaded clipboard and flicked through it, double checking a few last-minute entries. The flight was over, after all, and so I could relax my focus a bit.

The cockpit came to a standstill for a few moments. As the sound of the engine spooling down subsided, only the faint scratching of my pen racing along the empty lines of the daily flight documents could be heard. Another successful flight! Well, not quite… Complacency had set its devious claws into us by then, and fatigue had crafted a twisted scheme. It was never quite clear what brought about the next surprise, but I can tell you it was eye-opening, because, well, *there I wuz'*…

Breaking the short silence, my captain's voice almost startles me more than his frantic announcement, "We have a FIRE!" (Bear in mind this is paraphrased to save your eyes from the more . . . colorful wording actually used). I look up to the engine cowling of our PC12, but nothing seems out of the ordinary there. *Where's the fire?* I wonder.

I shift my eyes to the exhaust pipe on my side of the nose, and I am greeted by flames shooting past me, all the way to the door—bright orange and furious. Both of us go from standstill to full speed. In a split second we are both engaged in a battle against time, working as a team to vanquish this fire-breathing dragon that our airplane had just turned into.

The first words spoken are, "We need to evacuate!" But is that the safest thing to do? With flames blocking our natural egress through the main door, and with line crew personnel barely feet away from us on the ramp, a different plan is quickly devised. Our brains race against time, quickly reevaluating the situation. A new plan is proposed. "How about running the engine without injecting fuel, to snuff in the flames and cool it down?"

These crucial seconds of discussion were, in my opinion, the very heart of CRM. Both crew members offered solutions, evaluated and together acted on the best plan of action. The engine was later pronounced a total loss, but we protected the immediate safety of all occupants onboard the airplane as well as the well-being of the adjacent line personnel, while containing and neutralizing the threat.

This event led to what was, for me, a defining landmark in my aviation career. The ensuing investigation taught me that no matter how seasoned a pilot, there is always need to constantly strive to learn, improve, challenge and better oneself, both skill-wise and knowledge-wise.

The learning process will teach you more about yourself than you ever imagined, and allow you to become an inherent part of your team's success.

Author of The Pilot Factor*, Jean Denis Marcellin is currently a Citation captain for a major Canadian charter company and aircraft management business.*

His passion for Crew Resource Management (CRM) and life experience flows into his company, Plane&Simple Solutions, where he teaches effective leadership and communication skills promoting a safer cockpit for the student pilot to the airline professional.

Visit Mr. Marcellin's site at planesimplesolutions.com and contact him by email at jd.marcellin@gmail.com

Ron Rapp: Taming the Beast

Commercial Pilot—Aerobatic Pilot and Judge—Blogger

"Time for Plan B! But first I've got to make a Plan B."

Along with Mark L. Berry and Karlene Petitt, Ron Rapp is a member of our elite *Blogging in Formation* team.

A commercial Gulfstream IV pilot, aerobatic competitor and national judge, Ron brings his considerable general aviation flying experience to the table. This year, Ron's blog, *House of Rapp* (rapp.org) celebrated its 20th "blogiversary." Yes, he was one of the pioneers of blogging!

In this wild story, Ron learns the hard way that, if you can land a Pitts, you can land anything.

But first, you gotta land it.

What's your most memorable flight?

For me, it's a tough call; there are so many. The control jam in the middle of an aerobatic sequence? The electrical fire in a U-21A?

Perhaps one of several partial engine failures I've experienced could be considered most unforgettable.

Of course, not all my notable flights have centered around near-death experiences. There have been many joyous and poignant occasions as well: my first solo, first instrument approach to minimums in actual IMC, scattering the ashes of loved ones, taking an old friend for their last flight, introducing kids to the wonders of aviation, helping those in need through Angel Flight, and more.

There is one particular flight, however, which keeps coming back to me. It's hard to say that this is the most memorable, above and beyond all the others. But I can state with certainty that this is not a flight I'm likely to ever forget.

It was April of 2006, and for some masochistic reason I'd decided to get checked out in a Pitts S-2B. If you've never had the pleasure of flying one of these, it's the kind of airplane that can go from exhilarating to terrifying and back again in extremely short order. All of Curtis Pitts' designs have what you might call "personality." Depending on the quality if your last landing, of course, you might call it something else.

Something wholly inappropriate for polite company.

It's not like I was a neophyte when it comes to high-performance aerobatic tailwheel airplanes. I was already instructing in the mid-wing Extra 300, which has its own list of challenges. Even with the Extra 300 experience, though, the Pitts was a worthy challenge.

I'm actually surprised the FAA certified it at all. I mean, the fuel tank is inside the cockpit. And if the plane ever goes over on its back you won't be able to open the canopy and can easily end up covered with fuel if the tank gets crushed by the engine that sits directly in front of it.

A friend of mine actually did have to make an off-airport landing in his Pitts S-2B later that year. Yuichi was lucky — the fuel tank remained intact.

Like I said, the Pitts is a worthy challenge.

But once you've mastered — I mean really mastered — this airplane, I firmly believe you can fly anything. And I'm not the only one who thinks that. I once ran into a NASA astronaut in Las Vegas who said he'd taken the controls of many different flying machines ranging from gliders to helicopters to supersonic jets to the space shuttle, and in his opinion if you could land a Pitts you could land anything. Did I mention he was also a test pilot before he joined NASA?

Anyway, I'd been flying a series of dual flights in the Pitts with a fellow CFI and was doing well in the relatively benign wind conditions prevalent at John Wayne Airport (KSNA). I'd completed the full spin course in the airplane, including all upright and inverted spin modes, plus crossovers from upright to inverted and vice-versa. But I had yet to solo.

The day arrived to move the airplane out to Borrego Springs a the two-day training camp, which preceded the annual spring aerobatic contest.

No problem. The plan was for me to solo out there during the training camp. In many ways, Borrego was a better environment for it. A longer runway, less traffic, no wake turbulence concerns, and fewer distractions.

What could possibly go wrong?

The first flight at L08 was dual and honestly felt a little rough around the edges. The emphasis had gone from focusing exclusively on landing the airplane to flying competitive-level aerobatic sequences before doing so. Eventually it was determined that I was "good to go" and the next flight found me in the cockpit by myself for the first time.

To say I could feel the eyes of the world on me would be an understatement. The training camp was populated exclusively by tailwheel aerobatic pilots, and everyone was watching. I don't recall much about how the training session in the box went, but I'll never forget what happened next.

After vacating the box, I flew over the airport and entered right traffic for runway 8. By the time I reached pattern altitude, it was clear that the wind had picked up. A lot. Welcome to the desert! After turning final I noticed that the windsock indicated I'd be landing with a tailwind. So, I went around, congratulating myself for catching the change, and reentered for left traffic on runway 26.

Problem solved!

Or not. Oddly enough, the windsock on the *other* end of the runway was showing a tailwind there, too.

Another go-around.

Circling overhead, I took a careful look at the windsocks and noticed they were each pointing in different directions, and moving all over the place.

The turbulence had increased significantly, and the wind velocity at each sock seemed to be at least 20 knots because they were fully deflected.

Time for Plan B! But first I've got to make a Plan B.

I briefly thought about simply waiting it out, but that strategy doesn't work for long in a Pitts. I took off with about 15 gallons of fuel, and the airplane will burn through that in about 45 minutes.

I'd never encountered this before. Both ends of the runway were indicating tailwinds and the midfield area seemed to have a substantial, direct 90 degree crosswind. If you're not a tailwheel pilot, you might wonder what the big deal is. Assuming you've got enough runway — and at 5,011 feet, Borrego certainly is long — what's the hazard?

Tailwheel airplanes are directionally unstable on the ground, and landing in a tailwind means you'll lose rudder effectiveness (and therefore control) as you slow down after landing.

In most airplanes, the landing is "over" once you're on the ground. But the guys flying tailwheel aircraft know that touchdown is when the fun begins, as the aircraft tries to go everywhere except straight.

I radioed down to the ground to ask for an opinion on the conditions there at midfield and was told the winds were gusty and coming from various directions. They were seeing the same thing I was. Question is, what to do about it?

The suggestion came back, "Just pick a runway." Well, I've only got two to choose from. I elected to circle over the airport a couple more times. Then I realized things had indeed changed! The windsocks were all fully reversed. Both runways now indicated a headwind! I was starting to wonder if this was some sort of trick they played on pilots crazy enough to try and solo a Pitts. The aerobatic equivalent of asking for a "bucket of prop wash," as it were.

By now, I was starting to think more about fuel. Or the lack thereof.

In a Pitts, the fuel level is indicated by a simple tube connected to the fuselage tank. The turbulence had the fuel flowing up and down the tube, so it was hard to get a reading. And the thought of needing to divert to another airport meant I'd have to watch things carefully. Aside from a small residential airpark, there are no airports terribly close to Borrego Springs.

Another look at the windsocks. They've all reversed once again! Tailwinds on both runways. Hmmm. Suddenly, the wisdom of "just pick a runway" began to dawn on me.

I flipped a mental coin and reentered the pattern, bumping my head on the canopy over and over again and I descended on base and then final. The approach looked good. Real good, in fact. I kept expecting something nasty to happen, but it never did. I fought Mother Nature all the way down to the ground, floated for what seemed like an eternity, and made the softest, smoothest touchdown I'd ever experienced. "Am I on the ground? I think I'm on the ground...."

"Oh &#@*, I'm on the ground!" I realized.

The wind hit me from the right, but I danced on those pedals and kept it straight. Then the left, then the right again. The stick was all the way back and she was solidly on three wheels. Nothing left to do but keep it straight on the rollout.

But there was a gust from in front of the little red biplane, and it got light on the wheels in a big hurry. Airborne again, dammit! Okay, stay with it . . . re-flare . . . plenty of runway left . . . *squeak!* Or was it *plop!*?

Who cares! I did it. My goal was achieved: land a Pitts without breaking anything but a sweat.

As far as I was concerned, the entire week was a success at that point. I'd proved to myself that it was possible to coax, manhandle, and sweet-talk this red devil back down to Mother Earth.

After extracting myself from the cockpit, I went into the airport terminal (really nothing more than a semi-permanent trailer sitting on the ramp) and bent over the desk to see the digital ASOS wind readout. The direction was all over the place, but what really caught my eye was the velocity: gusting to more than 40 knots.

Borrego is like that. I recall being on the judging line once when a front passed through and you could actually see it coming. The wind shift on frontal passage was so strong that it broke a PVC pipe used in the shade structure over my head. I heard it but didn't see anything because my eyes were filled with sand.

In the southwestern U.S., these aerobatic contests are always held in the desert, and there's rarely a shortage of "sporty" wind conditions once afternoon hits.

I've had a few other notable experiences getting back on the ground after landing, but none quite as memorable as that first Pitts solo.

The legends are true, my friends: what doesn't kill you really does make you stronger.

Ron Rapp is an ATP-rated pilot with experience in more than 60 aircraft types, including tailwheels, aerobatics, formation flying, gliders, seaplanes, turboprops, business jets, warbirds, experimentals, radials, technologically advanced aircraft, and more. He's logged more than 7,500 hours over the past 20 years volunteering with Angel Flight, writing mile-long messages in the air as a SkyTyper, crop-dusting with ex-military King Airs, flying around the world in a Gulfstream IV, and tumbling through the air in his Pitts S-2B.

He's owned three aircraft (thankfully not all at the same time) and flown as an IAC aerobatic competitor up through the Advanced level. He's also an accredited National-level judge and his 2,500 hours of dual instruction include teaching recreational and competition-style aerobatics to numerous students in the Pitts, Extra, Decathlon, Eagle, other such aircraft.

Ron writes for AOPA's Opinion Leaders blog and his work has also appeared in Sport Aviation, Sport Aerobatics, Airscape, CPA Magazine, General Aviation News, Zocalo Public Square, California Political Review, NatGeoTV, KCRW, *and various other publications, podcasts, and television programs.*

He and his wife live in Orange County, California with their son and two evil–yet diabolically brilliant–Siamese cats.

SECTION 3: Pilots of the Caribbean (& Alaska)

Mallard formation during evacuation.
Note the telltale washboard swells of an approaching hurricane.
(See following story)

Gone with the Hurricane!
PART II: LEFT BEHIND
(Continued from Volume I)

Our world turned upside down

"Chaos reigned. Looting was rampant. Gunshots rang through the night. For two weeks, I carried a machete."

I wrote this story shortly after experiencing Hurricane Hugo in 1989. When I first published it on the blog years later, it coincided with the very week that Hurricane Sandy devastated the Eastern U.S. Seaboard.

The timing was a freak coincidence, and in no way did I intend to detract from the many hardships and sufferings experienced by survivors and victims of other Hurricanes such as Sandy, Katrina and Ivan. This is merely my story.

I can only hope that the rest of the "uninitiated" world will learn a lesson or two here about living through a hurricane, and also about the madness, mayhem and lawlessness that follows . . .

Backstory: When we last left our intrepid adventurers, a young Cap'n Aux had evacuated his Virgin Islands Seaplane Shuttle (VISS) Twin Otter to San Juan. In the confusion, girlfriend Julia was inadvertently left behind to fend for herself.

Category 5 hurricane Hugo scored a direct bullseye hit on the tiny island of St. Croix, U.S. Virgin Islands, then parked its blender over the island for eight solid hours.

All contact was lost with the island.

Three days later, the evacuees return in a scout plane, a Grumman Mallard amphib, to observe the devastation—and search for survivors. Including—Cap'n Aux prays—Julia.

We buzzed the island. Debris strewn everywhere. Nary a rooftop intact. The entire island, once a vast green jungle, lay brown and defoliated, as if the enemy had dropped napalm. The only boats not sunk were those washed ashore.

Boats cluttered the streets of downtown Christiansted.

People emerged from their battered homes and waved to us; we were their first contact from the outside world in two days.

Captain Rudy circled Christiansted Harbor, inspecting the bay for a safe water landing. He gently set down in the water, careful not to hit any flotsam from the newly sunk ships. Gingerly navigating between sunken ships, he taxied out of the water and up the VISS ramp.

TRIUMPHANT RETURN: Shuttle employees cheer our arrival, the first sign of civilization they'd seen in three days.

Seaplane Shuttle employees ran up and cheered; they hadn't known our fate any more than we had theirs.

I shared a tender reunion with Julia, who had survived unscathed.

The planes we left in St. Croix were not so lucky. They lay scattered across the ramp; twisted pieces of scrap. At the airport, I found, our remaining Twin Otter lay sprawled on its back, wings clipped at the root, landing gear sticking skyward like the legs of a dead horse.

Cap'n Aux invites Julia aboard.

Hugo claimed the lives of 25 people; no one we knew, thank goodness, was hurt. But each had a chilling horror story to tell.

———

Our apartment: Flooded, destroyed. But we were lucky. The only thing left standing in the apartment above us was the shower stall.

———

John, a Seaplane Shuttle mechanic, hid under a mattress in his bathroom. With a barometric altimeter, he dutifully recorded the pressure drop while his apartment fell to pieces around him.

At the height of the storm, he noted, the barometric pressure had plummeted over four inches below standard, the equivalent of 4,000' of altitude, and shattering the record for all previously recorded hurricanes.

Endangered species: The precious Grumman Mallard, now nearly extinct.

FO Chris's former residence

One boat owner, determined to stay with his ship, became a human cannonball as a gust hurtled him into the top of a palm tree. He crash-landed unharmed, if a bit dazed.

For the next two weeks, chaos reigned. Looting was rampant. Gunshots rang through the night. Gas and food became instant precious commodities. When driving around the island in "the Flaming Pumpkin," my bright orange Ford Fiesta "Island car" junker, I carried a machete.

That experience made me a true believer in the U.S. Constitution's Second Amendment, the Right to Bear Arms.

After the disaster, most of us moved stateside; leaves blown and scattered in the hurricane wind. Some stayed behind to rebuild their homes.

"The Flaming Pumpkin," my trusty island car, saves our bacon.

With our scant few possessions, Julia evacuated on a U.S. Army C-141 while I stayed behind for two weeks to help close the airline down.

Our crazy kitty Loco, a stray found in a local cantina, escaped back into the concrete wilderness from which she'd come, to once again fend for herself.

The Seaplane pilot gang, scattered in the hurricane wind. Represented at this table: future pilots for America West Airlines, USAirways, Delta, United and American Airlines.

For the past year, I had been a highfalutin' commuter airline captain, living worry free in paradise. Windsurfer dude by day, Cap'n by night. Now, I was once again a pilot pauper, with no poker game in sight to scam a new job (See "The Poker Game that Launched my Career" *There I Wuz! Volume I*)

Thousands flee Hugo; looting reported

Associated Press

CHARLESTON, S.C. — Hurricane Hugo's leading edge brought rain to the lower East Coast today, and thousands fled inland. The first of 1,000 soldiers sent by President Bush arrived in the Virgin Islands to quell looting in the storm's wake.

With landfall expected as early as tonight between Florida and North Carolina and the killer storm's winds rising to 110 mph, schools were closed, homes were boarded up, residents stocked up on emergency supplies and shelters opened.

Forecasters warned that waves could tower as much as 16 feet above normal because the hurricane could cross the coast at high tide, about 2:30 a.m. Rain of 5 to 10 inches was forecast.

The military brought aircraft inland and sent ships out to sea to ride out the storm, which has killed at least 25 people in the Caribbean with direct blows to Puerto Rico and the Virgin Islands.

South Carolina's governor declared an emergency and called out the National Guard to help thousands move inland. As many as 400,000 people were being evacuated from the coast in Georgia, where an emergency also was declared.

U.S. military police were sent to the Virgin Islands to reinforce U.S. marshals, FBI agents and armed Coast Guardsmen who were dispatched after police reportedly joined prison escapees and machete-armed mobs in looting on St. Croix.

The first contingent, about 75 soldiers led by a brigadier general, arrived this morning, secured the airport and set up a command center. It appeared to be the first time in more than 20 years that a president ordered active duty military personnel into the nation's streets.

I jumpseated home to Phoenix with my tail between my legs, once again pondering my future…

Julia begins the dig-out.

Confucius say: He who live in glass house should not reside in Hurricane Alley. Hurricane Sale! Everything must (or already did) go!

Clearing an escape path

Today, the Virgin Islands Seaplane Shuttle—that little airline in paradise —is no more. Gone with the hurricane, replaced by other intrepid seaplane operators.

The Islands just wouldn't be the same without one.

Now, St. Croix is largely the resort island it once was.

46

As naughty as little Hugo had been, his Mother has seen to it that the mess is cleaned up.

My only question: Where the HELL did that kitchen stove come from?!?!?!?!

LIfe Aquatic, and the Battle for Air Supremacy

This is a funny little ditty I wrote early on for the blog.

It begins with a true story: an aviation article about a near miss between an Air New Zealand airliner—and a shark.

Never mind that said shark was of the inflatable, remote-control drone-type. Regardless, a 15-foot Great White gunning for you at altitude had to be a somewhat harrowing experience for the flight crew!

Like anything Bill Murray—especially his quirky movie, *The Life Aquatic With Steve Zissou*—the humor in this short piece is both subtle and absurd. Not all get it. But I've found Mr. Murray to be one of the most brilliant comedians of our time, and I guess this is my attempt to try my hand at filling those big shoes.

Yes, it's silly, it's short, but for some reason it remains a personal favorite.

Last week aviation headlines were made when a near miss occurred between an Air New Zealand airliner…and a shark.

Yes, folks, you heard me right! Captain Sully's suicidal flocks of Airbus-downing Canadian geese got nuthin' on this aero-nautical predator. Nor, for that matter, does Jaws…

But what the unsuspecting traveling public doesn't know is that aviators have been battling aquatic fauna for aerial supremacy since Wilber Wright nearly lost his wing-warping right hand to a rabid nurse shark in 1906. And, suspiciously stricken from the annals of history, is Charles Lindbergh's confirmed testimony of his harrowing encounter, while flying at 10,000' on his historic transatlantic flight, with a school of killer jellyfish.

Yes, we pilot types have known all along about the vast conspiracy by the industry and world governments to coverup (no, not talking chemtrails) these close encounters of the marine kind.

Think dolphins are benign, cutsey things you pet at Seaworld? Guess again. Given the chance, a school of marauding bottlenose surfin' the jet stream will take out a modern airliner before you can say, "Flipper."

Even Cap'n Aux himself, while flying the Alaska bush out of Juneau, AK, had a literal run-in at altitude with a two pound Chinook salmon in 1988. Well, actually, while delivering Tlingit locals and logging supplies to Hoonah in my treetop-cruising Cessna 207, I startled an enormous bald eagle who dropped its freshly caught load, which was shredded by my prop and splattered across the windshield.

Talk about a bad day for Mr. Salmon!

Author confession: ok, so the salmon midair didn't happen to me, but guess what: it did happen!

Excerpt from AlaskaAirblog.com:

Windshield Sushi
Alaska Airlines jet really did hit a fish in midair

The airplane that hit a fish is one of the most legendary stories in Alaska Airlines lore.

Like all great fish tales, the size of the fish grows with every telling, but the story that made headlines around the world in 1987 is completely true. (Although it probably didn't help that newspapers published the story on April Fool's Day.)

On March 30, 1987, an Alaska Airlines 737-200 lifting off from Juneau had a close encounter of the aquatic kind, colliding with a large fish. The fish was gripped in the talons of an eagle that had crossed flight paths with the plane. The eagle must have decided that playing "chicken" with a 737 wasn't going to end well, and quickly changed direction.

"In the process, the eagle either voluntarily released its meal or the rapid turn ripped it out of its claws," Anchorage-based Alaska Airlines pilot Captain Mac af Uhr wrote in a 2005 story about the incident. "In one of those 'I cannot believe this is happening to me' moments, the two pilots (Bill Morin and Bill Johnson) watched the fish fall toward the aircraft as if in slow motion."

"Did we just hit what I think we hit?" Morin reportedly said over the radio, as the fish thumped the aircraft just behind the cockpit window. The eagle apparently escaped injury. The fish became windshield sushi, confirmed upon inspection at the aircraft's next stop in Yakutat.

"They found a greasy spot with some scales, but no damage," Paul Bowers, Juneau airport manager, told The Associated Press at the time.

Morin would later estimate that the fish was about 12- to 18-inches long, and that it may have been a Dolly Varden.

SECTION 4: Adventure Travel

My buddy Mark McCabe (L.) and I (center), at the Pyramids of Giza, outside Cairo, Egypt, circa 1994

Tawni Waters: Marilyn Monroe in Mexico
(OR, HOW I MADE MY WAY ACROSS MEXICO USING ONLY MY BOOBS)

Author Tawni Waters. Photo courtesy of Joe Birosak

"A snake of terror coiled around my heart. I was in the wrong city."

No, this isn't "literary erotica" slipped surreptitiously into an otherwise PG-rated adventure travel book. This is an utterly hysterical story by famed writer Tawni Waters, author of the best-selling novel, *Beauty of the Broken*. In 2015, *Beauty* won the International Literacy Association Award for Young Adult Literature—one of the most prestigious literary prizes in the world.

Back in the late 90's, I was honored to read an early copy of the manuscript that would become Ms. Waters' classic, *Beauty of the Broken*. Dare I say, I stopped writing for several years after that, as her genius made me feel like I was still learning my ABC's.

Ms. Waters is a noted travel writer as well, having beat out two Pulitzer Prize winners to capture the Grand Prize in *2010's Best Travel Writing* with her story, *Ashes of San Miguel*.

Ms. Waters is one of the greatest writers of our time. She writes not only with an entertaining yet deep profundity, but also with a rare gift of humor, as you'll soon see. Every piece she's ever written leaves you crying with joy, and laughing with sorrow. And contemplating the meaning of life for days.

Yes, she's that good.

I am slouched in a Starbucks in San Miguel de Allende, Mexico, but the only things here to remind me that I am not in America are:

A. The fact that I just had a very hard time ordering my latte.

B. The fact that I just paid a pretty, wide-eyed child $10 for five Chiclets.

C. The fact that a man just came over and asked me to put a peso in his can, and when I did, he slapped a Whinny-the-Pooh sticker directly on my right boob.

I am here because:

A. Starbucks is the only place in town with electrical outlets that jive with my computer cord.

B. I am scared witless and need to be reminded that the whole wide world is not made up of serial killers bent on raping me for sport and harvesting my kidneys for profit.

Say what you will about Starbucks. Say that it is the face on the greedy corporate American monster gobbling up the whole world. Say that every time you arrive in Bangladesh or Rome or Tel Aviv and see a Starbucks staring out at you from its place beside ancient ruins, it makes you want to fall to your knees and weep. Say that, frankly, Starbucks coffee stinks.

And I get you, I do. Theoretically. But honestly, for my part, today, Starbucks makes me feel safe. In fact, whenever I arrive in Bangladesh, or Rome, or Tel Aviv, Starbucks always makes my disoriented, hapless American ass feel safe. So I hobble in and order a latte in broken sentences, to make me feel somehow connected to the continent that spawned me. This makes me part of the problem, I suppose, a cell in the great monster. If Starbucks is the modern equivalent of Roman bread and circuses, color me plied. Throw stones, if you must, at me and my Starbucks frequenting ways, but today, I need to feel safe. As I mentioned earlier, I am quite convinced the world is peopled with serial killers intent upon raping me and harvesting my kidneys.

The seeds of my terror were planted in Starbucks-infested America. I was leaving for San Miguel the next day, and I spoke to my Mommy, who loves me very much and demonstrates her love in a variety of ways, but most often, by warning me of danger. Usually, the danger is nonexistent, but she still warns me. Last week, she warned me that I was going to get Hepatitis B because I got fake fingernails. (I don't get the connection. When pressed, neither did she. But she was still quite adamant in her warning.) The reason I got fake fingernails is that, in addition to being a writer, I am also an actress, and as such, I am in a production in which I play a Marilyn Monroe-esqe diva of sorts. Now, blond-wigged and fake-nailed, I am heading to San Miguel to grace some four-hundred-year old building with a week of performances.

So, back in Starbucks-ville, I called my Mommy to say goodbye, and her final words to me were something along these lines: "Don't forget the American women that are being raped and dismembered in Mexico." My Mommy's version of "Safe travels, *Via con Dios*, etc." I didn't think much of it at the time. "Thanks, Mom. I'll remember," I said. And packed my stilettos and headed out to play a diva on some San Miguel stage.

All went beautifully the morning of my travels. From Albuquerque, I flew, hassle free, into Houston and connected to a plane that was to take me to Leon, where my director was going to meet me with a car to drive me to our lodgings in nearby San Miguel. Easy cheesy, right? Even if I had never been to San Miguel before, it would have been a fool proof travel plan. And I had been to San Miguel. I had spent a beautiful month in that city, wandering the cobblestone streets, basking in the morning sun in the *jardin*, buying handmade dolls and Chiclets and flowers from beautiful women in Kool-Aid colored shawls. I knew these streets. They were mine. As I said, a fool proof plan.

Whoever made up the phrase "fool proof plan" did not take me into account. No plan is proofed enough for this fool. This fool somehow managed to get on the wrong plane, undetected. And landed in a completely unfamiliar locale and thought only this: "Wow, they must have redone the airport." And sat there outside customs blithely reading a book, waiting for her director, while a cluster of Mexican airport officials ogled her. This fool tried to act tough, so as to dissuade the Mexican men from their ogling, only this fool is kinda crappy at acting tough, as she is usually bumbling around, bumping into large, valuable pottery artifacts and repeating, ad nauseum, her mantra, which is, "*¿Habla da English?*" (Just like that.) Because even though this fool has a few years of Spanish classes under her belt, she has retained a vocabulary of maybe a hundred words and a few useful phrases. ("*¿Donde esta el bano? ¿Un tequila por favor? Yo quiero un botella de agau frio. Tu gato es muy bonita. ¿Cuanto es?*)

It was only after my director failed to arrive that I began to suspect something was desperately wrong. I looked out the window and saw lots of palm trees. I didn't remember seeing lots of palm trees in Leon. I noticed that the airport restaurant was much, much larger than it had once been, and was on the opposite side of the building. They had added wireless internet since my last visit, if the signs were to be believed, though I couldn't access it because I had no adaptor for my computer plug. They had moved the bank machine. Also, the bathrooms were much cleaner. Oh no. A snake of terror coiled around my heart and squeezed.

I was in the wrong city.

When a girl realizes she is in a foreign country alone and does not speak the language and does not know where she is, she gathers her wits. Well, first, she hunkers down behind a potted fern and weeps. Then, she gathers her wits. Which are easy to gather, because there aren't really many of those wit things running around in said girl's head. (Obviously. She got on the wrong plane to a foreign country.) The girl whispers things to herself, bits of wisdom. "What would Jesus do? One two three four, I declare a thumb war. I before E except after C, and when sounded like AY as in NEIGHBOR and WEIGH."

Ms. Waters in a decidedly happier mood. Exploring the pyramids at Teotihuican, with nary a kidney harvester in site.

Then she takes stock of her resources. What do I have that can help me in this situation? Language skills are not on that list. Nor are navigational skills. Money? Not much. Friends? *Nada.* Cell phone? No signal. Internet? No plug. A girl goes down here list of assets, and finally, she concludes, *I have boobs.*

This is so un-feminist of her, she knows, but her mother's warning is ringing in her ears, and it is already three in the afternoon, and she has to get to her lodgings before nightfall, or she will be raped and hacked apart. Also, she has a show to do tomorrow, and if she doesn't get there, even if the serial killers don't harvest her kidneys, her director will.

So the girl goes into the bathroom and plumps up her boobs and applies some lipstick and sashays back out of the restroom, on over to the Mexican airport officials who have been ogling her. She whispers, sultrily, using all of the Marilyn Monroe-esque know-how she has garnered during her acting career, "*¿Habla da English?*"

Then she trips over a pottery artifact.

The officials are all over it. They help her up and restore the artifact to its rightful place. They say, "No, no, no English," but they take the girl by the hand and across the airport to a corpulent airport official who does, in fact, *habla da English*. She looks like a movie star with a bunch of body guards until she trips over another artifact. Then she just looks like a witless fool. Which, we have already established, she is.

She explains her plight to the English speaking official, and he explains it to the non-English speaking entourage, and they all nod knowingly and chatter amongst themselves, after which take the girl back into their office.

Oh crap, now they are going to rape me and dismember me, she thinks. But they don't. Instead, they spend the next half hour finding the girl the quickest route from Ixtapa (which is where she is, it turns out) to San Miguel. This involves a cab ride to a bus depot, a four hour bus ride to a city called Morelia, and then another two hour bus ride to San Miguel. Airport officials beg the witless girl to spend the night. The girl pictures being hacked apart by said airport officials, panics, apologizes, thanks them profusely ("*Gracias, lo siento*," is one of her phrases), and runs to a waiting cab, which befuddled airport officials order to take girl to bus depot.

This boob thing is working out, so girl thinks she will use it again at the bus depot. But the bus depot holds no ogling officials, only flies, Fanta dealers, and females. The females are not amused by the girl's antics. No, they are not, but somehow, she manages to convey she wants to go to Morelio. "*Un boleta a Morelio por favor*." She says this with a terrible accent and great gusto, only her request is greeted with inquiries, rapidly phrased Spanish questions which the girl doesn't understand. The ticket selling females do not *habla da* English. Worse, they recognize the witless girl for what she is. Suddenly, boobs are useless weapons. The witless girl has been disarmed. Still, even though the ticket selling females mock the girl in angry Spanish, they sell her a ticket.

She slumps into the waiting room, which smells slightly of urine and boasts a small television, playing Mexican soap operas. The girl struggles to understand the dialogue, trying to hone her language skills for the bus ride ahead. She pictures boarding a rattle trap van held together with bailing wire. She pictures being approached by a serial killer with a scalpel in his holster.

(Mexican serial killers wear holsters.) She pictures pleading for her life. What would she say? She watches the soap opera intently. "¡*No, señor!* ¡*No, no!*" That's it. She has her line. Any actress knows that getting your lines down is just the beginning. After that, it's all in the delivery. Should she say, "¡*No señor!*" or "¡*No, señor!*" Probably the second one. It will emphasize the killer's humanity. Make him think twice before her takes her kidneys. It will remind the girl's killer she is more than a host for organs. She is a human being, damn it! He will fall to his knees, weeping. "*Lo siento!*" he will scream. "*Lo siento!*"

Luckily, when the witless girl boards two wrong buses, the ticket takers are men, who do not *habla da English* but are clearly moved by her witlessness and her boobs. They look at her with pity, like she is a brain damaged child, and help her off the wrong buses, and finally, onto the right one. The bus is not what the girl expected. It is air conditioned and comfortable, and she gets a whole row to herself. And a free Fanta. Score!

As the bus lurches off for Morelia, the girl drinks her delicious Fanta and starts to think of this whole thing as adventure. She listens to "Born to Run" on her iPod while watching Mexico slither by outside her window like a gorgeous green snake. She sees thick climbing vines and pink flowers with faces as big as her own. She watches soldiers sipping Coca Colas under thatched roofs and goats eating tires inside brightly painted yards. She smiles at a raisin faced old woman leading a plump, grape faced girl by the hand along a dusty path. She waves at taco vendors dancing to their radios. One of them waves back at her, and she laughs, listening now to Roger Clyne's song, "I Speak Your Language." These people may not understand a word she says, but they understand her. At least the men do. They speak the universal language of boobs.

All is going well. At this rate, the girl will be in Morelio in no time. When she gets there, she will buy another ticket and board another air conditioned bus to San Miguel. It's all so easy. She should do this more often, and look, there is a red bridge over glassy water with the sun setting behind it. How glorious! Look at the orange peel colored sunset being reflected back to the sky. The girl starts to scribble in her notepad, which she carries in her pocket for just such moments of inspiration. "The sky is looking in a mirror," she writes. "The sky—"

Screech! The bus lurches to a halt. As her mother instructed, the girl remembers the American women that are being raped and dismembered. The girl imagines bandits boarding the bus and zips up her coat. The girl wipes off her lipstick and pulls her hair into a tight ponytail. The girl slumps over, puffs out her stomach, and tries to look as un-boobalicious as humanly possible. She can't speak to the bandits with words, but she can speak to them with her eyes. "I do not want to be raped and harvested!" she wills her eyes to scream. "I am a mother, for God's sake!" *Yo* means I. *Madre* is mother. She can even say this in Spanish. "¡*No, señor. Yo madre!*" Which may be taken to mean something like, "Your momma!" which could further enrage the killer, but she will have to take her chances.

The bus driver comes back and fires off something, very quickly, in Spanish. The girl picks up a few words. *Buenos dias. Lo siento.* Bus. Luggage. Then a passenger starts yelling. He says something about *mi familia*. Barely able to breathe, the trembling girl tries to use these clues to understand the content of the conversation. She comes up with this.

BUS DRIVER: *Buenos dias.* I am sorry to inform you that the bus has been taken by serial-killing bandits who are now rifling through your luggage, looking for valuables. Soon, they will board the bus, rape all the American women, dismember them, and harvest their organs.

PASSENGER: That boobalicious woman is obviously an American! Take her and leave my family!

The girl begins to weep. She wants to ask if any of the other passengers *habla da English* and can translate the bus driver's announcement, but she knows the killers are targeting Americans and doesn't want to give herself away. The bus sits for an hour. The passenger gets off the bus, ostensibly to beg the bandits for mercy for his wife and children. He comes back smelling like smoke. So they must be setting the luggage on fire now. It's only a matter of time. "Born to Run" is little comfort. "I Speak Your Language" is even less. Girl listens to another Clyne song. "Mercy, mercy, mercy may I be," he says. She thinks she will focus on the lines of this song as her organs are harvested. Maybe it is a parting gift from God, like that scene in Braveheart when Mel Gibson is being disemboweled and looks into the eyes of the smiling little boy for comfort. The girl looks out the window and whispers a prayer. To God or her dead daddy. Maybe to both of them. "Daddy, get me to San Miguel in one piece."

The bus lurches, then moves forward. The passengers make cheering noises. The girl weeps again, with relief this time. It is dark now. The air conditioning on the bus works, but the lights do not. The girl sits in her seat and prays in the blackness, fervently. The other passengers fall asleep, but she will not be lulled into a false sense of security. She will not rest.

It turns out the ogling men in the Ixtapa airport were wrong. With the bandit debacle, the bus ride takes six hours, give or take. By the time the bus pulls into Morelia, a lemon wedge moon is hanging in the sky, and the girl wishes she had toothpicks with which to prop her eyelids open. She is weary, but she cannot sleep, not until she is safely tucked away in her director approved bed in San Miguel, protected from the probing scalpels of organ harvesters. She hobbles off the bus, retrieves her luggage (which is mercifully unburned), and staggers into the Morelia bus depot. It is peopled by female ticket sellers, which doesn't make much of a difference at this point, because the girl is slightly stinky and anything but boobalicious. She manages to ask for a ticket to San Miguel de Allende, and the woman behind the counter rattles off a bunch of words, one of which the girl understands. *Mañana.*

Tomorrow.

The girl chokes back a sob. She cannot, *cannot* sleep here alone in this strange city. She pictures all those CSI episodes where people are hacked apart in hotel rooms. Her mother's warning merges with the images.

Crying again, she stumbles to a taxi stand. "*¿Cuanto es un taxi a San Miguel de Allende?*" she manages, wiping tears and snot away with the backs of her knuckles. The man behind the taxi stand laughs, but another man, a driver, doesn't. He is old and stooped and he reminds the girl of her father, of what he might look like now had he lived into old age. The driver looks at the girl, not unkindly, and says, "You safe?" She shrugs. "*Sí.*"

"Eight hundred pesos," he says, which is eighty dollars for a two hour ride. The girl knows the man is saving her ass, and she wants to kiss him. "*Gracias,*" she whispers, in a voice completely unsultry, no trace of Marilyn Monroe. "*Gracias, senior. Gracias.*" She climbs into the cab, and as the driver pulls into the street, the girl sees on a cinderblock wall the word "angel" scrawled in red ink. And it may be the unfamiliar Mexico air and exhaustion going to her head, but the girl wonders if God is trying to tell her something.

Her angel tries to talk to her as he drives, though between the two of them, the only word they seem to have in common is *agua*. Once the angel realizes this, every time he sees water, he points to it and kindly says, "*¡Agua! Bonita!*"

"*Sí,*" says the girl. "*Agua es muy bonita.*" And the angel smiles.

And so they go on like that, commenting enthusiastically on the beauty of the water. The girl notices that the air smells like smoke, and in the distance, she notices the orange eyes of fires burning holes in the night. She wants to ask her angel what these fires are for, but she can't find the words. The girl finally sleeps, and hours later, she wakes up to the sound of her angel's voice.

"See, lady? San Miguel de Allende."

When she opens her eyes, she sees the cobblestone streets lined with brightly painted doors, and she warms at the thought that she knows what is behind some of those doors. Some of the men and women sleeping behind those doors would recognize her face if they saw it. They might even say her name. Tawni.

Though her terror still lingers like a coiled snake in her belly, Tawni understands the proverbial impulse to kiss the ground, because this is the safest she has felt in many hours. These streets are hers, at least compared to the streets she has been bumping along all day. The angel finds another cabbie and pays him to lead the way to Tawni's *casa*, the address for which she has scrawled on a bit of paper. The angel carries her luggage to the door and when she offers to tip him, he runs his fingers through his thinning gray hair and shakes his head, smiling.

"*Gracias, senior,*" Tawni calls to his retreating back. "*Tu es un angel.*" Which she knows is wrong. But suddenly, it doesn't matter if her Spanish is bad or good. It just matters that she says what she needs to say.

"*De nada,*" calls the angel.

"It's not nothing. It's everything," Tawni wants to tell him, but by the time she finds the words, he has driven off under the lemon-wedge moon.

Author Tawni Waters is a writer, actor, and gypsy.

Her first novel, Beauty of the Broken, *published by Simon Pulse in 2014, won the International Reading Association Award for Young Adult Literature, and was also named an Exceptional Book of 2015 by the Children's Book Council. Her first poetry book,* Siren Song, *was released in the same year.*

Her work has been published in myriad journals, magazines, and anthologies, including Best Travel Writing 2010, Bridal Guide Magazine, Ft. Lauderdale Sun-Sentinel, Albuquerque Journal, and Blood Lotus. *She regularly contributes to* Burlesque Press.

She teaches workshops and retreats at various universities and conferences throughout the US.

In her spare time, she talks to angels, humanely evicts spiders from her floorboards, and plays Magdalene to a minor rock god.

Around the World in 80 Jumpseats

Originally submitted for publication to Smithsonian Air & Space Magazine. (They never got around to it, so their loss is our gain!)

Tired of the daily commute to work? You say you live in Long Beach and the trek to downtown L.A. takes two hours?

You wimp. That's peanuts to an airline pilot. The phrase *commuting to work* takes on a whole new meaning for the Chicago-based pilot whose spouse, kids and lawn mower are way back in Chattanooga, Tennessee.

In every airliner cockpit, there is at least one "jumpseat." This seat is required so that FAA inspectors or Check Airman can occasionally fly along with line pilots for regular flight checks.

Apparently, by Federal law, these jumpseats must be designed to be less comfy than a bed of nails. I am convinced they were designed either by sadistic dentists, or line pilots hoping to keep said flight checks to a minimum.

When not in official use, these extra seats—however horrid—have become the commuting pilot's life blood. As a professional courtesy, airlines regularly tote each other's pilots to and from work and home with this golden throne. Hey, how else do you think we get to share each other's company gossip?

Fortunately, when the cabin is less than full, the commuter is allowed access to a more sane cabin seat. Yes, even a coach seat is preferable to the cruel chair up front!

As an airline pilot, I've regularly trodden to and from work on that great car pool lane in the sky, logging nearly as many hours in back of the cockpit door as in front of it. As a Phoenix, Arizona native, I've commuted to and from work in Albuquerque, Denver, and Washington, DC.

Wiki: *A jump seat (or jumpseat), in aviation refers to an auxiliary seat for individuals — other than normal passengers — who are not operating the aircraft.[1] In general, the term 'jump seat' can also refer to a seat — in any type of vehicle — which can fold up out of the way; vehicles include carriages, automobiles, vans, buses, fire tenders, and taxicabs. The term originated in the USA circa 1860 for a movable carriage seat.*

A320 Primary Jumpseat

But even that's nothing. I recall the Boeing 727 captain for Pan Am (God rest the company's soul) who used to commute twice a week from Bozeman, Montana . . . to Munich, Germany. Or one of my recent first officers, who commutes from Phoenix, Arizona . . . to Chang Mai, Thailand.

When in uniform and sitting in the passenger cabin, I always feel like I'm on stage. At the slightest bump or klunk, white knucklers nervously glance to me with a, "Was that normal?" look. To calm their nerves, I always flash them a reassuring smile. But I'm always tempted to grab the arm rests, bug out my eyes and shout, "What the hell was that!"

My God, they'd panic.

Pilots are notoriously cheap (yours truly included), and have exploited the jumpseat privilege for leisure travel as well. Like doctors and lawyers, pilots enjoy virtually for free the fruits of their profession. But, before salivating with envy over the perk, remember that there ain't no such thing as a free inflight lunch. Pilots have either sacrificed years in the military, or in civilian flight schools (or both), and spent tens of thousands of dollars to get that "free" lunch.

Though the jumpseating pilot may be on vacation, tasteful dress and impeccable behavior is still required. If not in uniform, the pilot must often wear suit and tie, or at least "business casual"—and certainly no imbibing, either. White knuckle flyers, always looking for a bad omen, tend to spook upon glimpsing a cockpit crewmember decked in Bermudas, tank top and beachcombers, sipping a Piña Colada and flirting with the flight attendant.

Besides stringent dress codes, jumpseating has evolved other traditions and protocol as well. For instance, after the captain approves the jumpseat request, the traveler must always thank him personally. Once this is done, the jumper is often invited to take a seat in the cabin, if any are available. A jumper who fails to thank the captain may be asked to step outside—at cruise.

Another tradition is—surprise!—common courtesy. The jumpseater is nothing more than a high class hitchhiker, a freeloader who can be kicked off the train at the slightest sign of ingratitude. Woe to the cocky pilot who, with a condescending sneer, demands a jumpseat ticket from an already overburdened gate agent. Somehow, the paperwork always seems to lose itself in the honeycomb of the podium . . . only to be found a few seconds after the plane has pushed back.

The jumpseat may be uncomfy, but it makes for one helluva window seat!

All travelers could learn a lesson here, too: no matter how many connections you've missed, how many bags you've lost, no matter how many coffees have scalded your privates from a well-timed trounce through turbulence, never, ever piss off a gate agent—your ticket may be "inadvertently misplaced," too!

Contrary to the traveling public, who normally books flights fourteen-plus days in advance and rigidly sticks to the travel agency itinerary, the jumpseating pilot wings it (scuz the pun).

For example, let's say you've just finished a gruelling four day flight schedule that dumps you off (only ten minutes late) in Podunk, New York, and you've got to get back to LA for little Julia's 3rd birthday. As the turbofans wind down, you race through the Airplane Shutdown Checklist, throw your Jepps navigation charts into the flight kit, grab your overnight bag, shout "See-ya!" to the crew with whom you just lived through four days of toil, dash off the flight deck and fly like, well, O. J. through the terminal to the gate for the direct flight from Podunk to LAX.

Of course, it's gone. Pushing back, in fact, right before your bloodshot eyes and slumping shoulders, having departed exactly on time (you arrived ten minutes late, remember?)

Now comes the game I call, Airline Hopscotch.

You frantically search the nearest Departure screen for the quickest way outta here . . .

"Let's see, in twenty minutes there's a Delta out of Gate twelve direct to Chicago, and from there I could connect with United to San Francisco, but American goes to Dallas in an hour, and from there I could take USAir to Phoenix then Southwest to LAX. Or else I could . . . .

You get the picture.

Anywhere, at anytime, your grand scheme of cross-country connections could be shot down like Canadian geese through an Airbus turbofan. The jumpseat is typically first-come-first-served, so if another pilot makes it ahead of you, it's time to recalculate. Weather, mechanical problems or even a missing inflight meal could delay you ten, twenty, ninety agonizing minutes or more, and your whole itinerary augers in, flaming. (By the way, it has been scientifically proven that the time of delay on Flight One is inversely proportional to the connection time to Flight Two—the shorter the connect, the longer the delay.)

Okay, so you made it on the United to Chicago. Now you can breathe a sigh of relief and happily sip an orange juice back in coach. But wait! You've arrived an hour late and missed the connection to San Francisco.

Now it's time revise the plan of attack. Time to connect the dots through a few more terminals, cities and airlines. The old joke, "I just flew in, and boy are my arms tired!" rings sadly true when one must suddenly tote armloads of carry-ons from Terminal A to the connection in Terminal E.

Fortunately, today's technology has allowed commuting-pilot types to finally throw away pounds and pounds of airline timetable connection books, and simply use an app or two.

This leads us to another aspect of airline jumpseating: traveling light. This is mandatory. No U Haul-sized checked baggage allowed—you never know if you'll make it home to LAX, or end up camping out in the concrete jungle of plastic chairs in JFK.

A word of caution for those ground-pounders bold enough to entertain the idea of jumpseating illegally: last year, wannabe-jumpseater Philippe Jernnard was quickly nabbed in the cockpit of an airliner when he posed as a deadheading Air France pilot. He merely wanted to avoid the cramped quarters of Coach and get a free upgrade. Instead, he faces Federal charges.

Still tempted? Better stop and read *Catch Me if You Can*, the true story of infamous con man Frank Abignale. In it, Abagnale explains the difficulties of jumpseating when does not know the ritual or the lingo.

Fake airline I.D. in hand, Abagnale posed as a deadheading pilot to travel cross-country on a jumpseat. When asked by a "fellow" pilot, "What equipment you on?" The Normally the quick-witted con man, Abignale froze. Clueless to the fact that this industry buzzword equipment meant airplane, he replied hopefully, "Uh, General Electric!"

As Abignale and Jernnard both learned, a landlubber posing as a pilot stands out like a ticking Samsonite.

I Can Order a Drink in Ten Languages

"U N O   M A S CERVEZA,   POR FAVOR!"
—Spanish

My name is Eric. And I can order a drink in ten languages.

The world is a Disneyland made just for *you*. And if you don't take maximum advantage of this maxim while riding this big, giant ball, you're missing out on, well, one helluva a ball, and a *world* of adventure.

And I'm not talking two weeks' room service at the Vegas Belagio or the Park Central Ritz. Who needs another vacation filled with nothing but smoky slot machines, poolsides and inroom movies?

Ok, that's got it's place, too, but my point is if you're gonna make the effort to turn off the TV, get off the couch and out the door, then go *do something!* We're on a quest for *stories* here. We're shooting for *life lessons.*

But there are definitely some important caveats to winging it the do-it-yourself, adventure travel way.

"EIN BIER BITTE."
—German

My favorite trip is throwing on a backpack, throwing a dart at a map, and waking up there the next morning.

This certainly makes for some zany misadventures and dicey moments. But, you gotta understand. I grew up in a Leave it to Beaver world. No drama, no trauma, never moved, nary a tragedy. This made for a stable childhood, but filled me with wanderlust.

As a young pilot, I deliberately bounced all over the globe while climbing the aviation ladder.

I've flown Grand Canyon tours and the Alaska bush, captained for a seaplane operation in the Virgin Islands, and driven four-engine turboprops into Steamboat Springs STOLport, Colorado.

On days off, I'd race out the door for some random world locale, armed with nothing more than a backpack and a vague idea of destination.

"MO IPPON BIRU KUDASAI."
—Japanese

Sadly, we U.S. citizens all too often personify the "ugly American" while traveling abroad with our clueless, bull-in-a-china shop ways. Learning just a tad of another's language goes a long way to dispell this well-earned stereotype.

My college passion was Japanese. I learned enough to chat all day long with a smokin' Tokyo native on my very first trip. But, more than that, it taught me *appreciation* and *respect* for other cultures.

Learn English, Spanish and French, and you got 70+% of the world covered. Mandarin Chinese, 90%. A month or two before your trip, study the most basic of language lessons: "Hello, my name is . . .", "where is the . . .", "how much for . . .", etc. Or, if you really just don't have the time, then at least learn this one, simple phrase: "Another drink, please."

One simple phrase wouldn't seem to get you very far in any language, but the fact that you *made the effort* to speak a native's language most often charms them into being friendly and helpful.

And maybe even get you a free beer.

"UN VA CIE VOUS PLAIT."
—French

Eh, except for the French. They got damn good wine, but they'll turn up their nose in disgust at your butchering of their language. But, hell, they'd do that anyway. So, unless you devote much of your youth to mastering the nuances of the Parisian tongue, you'd be better off learning, say, Spanish. Or confining your use of pigeon French to the outer colonies.

"SHI SHI."
—Chinese

(OK, it really means "Thank you," but you get the idea)

From atop a camel, I've seen the sunrise over the Great Pyramids of Giza. I've Eurailed through Europe and backpacked through Japan. I've partied at Munich Oktoberfest, ice climbed and snowboarded the Swiss Alps, snorkeled Thailand and dived the Great Barrier Reef. I've kissed the Wailing Wall in Jerusalem, the Blarney stone in Dublin, and a Swedish flight attendant in Frankfurt. I once spent a week in a tiny Venezuelan fishing village, hours from any phone, paved road or English speaker. My favorite world locales are: Kyoto, Interlaken, Venice . . . .

And any tiny fishing village with no phone, paved road or English.

"ISA PA NGANG BEER!"
— Tagalog (The Philippines)

Just like Disneyland, no matter how much you've seen, there's so much more. And if my little bucket list has inspired you to put down the remote and see the world first hand, then you'd also best learn the *second* most important phrase:

"DONDE ESTA EL BANO, POR FAVOR?"
—Spanish
"VOZEN DIE TOILETTEN BITTE?"
—German
"OTEARAI WA DOKO DESU KA?"
—Japanese
"UE LE LOU, SIE VOUS PLAIT?"
—French
"SAAN ANG KUBETA?"
—Tagalog

English Translation: "Where is the bathroom, please?"

SECTION 5: By Popular Demand

A few of my most popular works

Top 10 Things to Never Say to a Pilot

This 2014 blog post *blew doors* on all the competition, bagging traffic ten times its closest contender. While I've never been about numbers, this particular post truly went "viral."

Since then, I've heard from many a pilot for whom this post rings true.

Below is a list of lines that, for an airline pilot, sound like nails on a chalkboard.

Most of the statements carry an unintended yet implied insult that keeps the pilot grumbling for hours afterward. If you're in the profession and have been on the receiving end of one of these, you know exactly what I'm talking about.

Of course, the majority of the statements or questions are innocent and carry no malice. They simply come from an innate misunderstanding of the profession, and are not intended to cause insult.

For you landlubbers, however, I encourage you to bite your tongue before uttering one of these pax faux pas, and consider rephrasing the question . . .

Or, better yet, use the onboard wifi to Google the answer!

10. What route do you fly?

This one baffles me, but it's the most common question we pilots ever get. This seems like a throwback to the golden age of the railway, gone now for nearly 100 years, when trains could only go where tracks took them.

Look, an airplane doesn't have this limit. A mile of runway will take you anywhere in the world!

Of course, what people are really asking is, *Where* do you fly—short hops, Domestic, or International?

Once again, however, the question can carry an unintended insult: the implication being the shorter the hop, the lesser the pilot you are.

To answer your question, once and for all: my routes are up and down, and all over the place! Well, that, and: U.S. Domestic, Canada, Mexico, and a little into Central America.

Fellow pilot-blogger-author Mark L. Berry wrote a song with the exact same phrase. (Yep, it's universally annoying!)

See: *What Route Do You Fly?* marklberry.com/what-route-do-you-fly-2/

9. Are you a pilot or a copilot?

Grr…bang, zoom, to the moon, Alice!

Like most in this list, it's not so much the question, but the implied insult.

First of all, the term "copilot" carries a false implication: that one is sort of a "pilot in training" or an "apprentice."

Absolutely, 100% WRONG!

Photo courtesy Brent Owens of Fixedwingbuddha.com

EVERYONE up front in that cockpit is 100% trained, qualified, and experienced enough to Captain the ship. They have all the required flight ratings and experience.

The SOLE reason the Captain is in command: s/he has more Company Seniority—not necessarily more experience—than the other fully qualified pilots in the cockpit.

Do us a favor and use the proper terminology: Captain and First Officer.

9.1 Corollary: You're the copilot? Do you wanna be a pilot some day?

See answer above.

And excuse me while I punch you in the face.

9.2 Corollary 2.0: Some day, do you wanna fly for the big airlines (variation: big airplanes/ big jets/ International)?

Nearly every pilot in the business hopes to fly for the biggest, bestest, worldwidest airlines, for the top pay and position, flying the biggest toys. But we are all at different points in our careers working up the ladder, and completely at the mercy of this fickle business. We are either on our way to that dream spot, or got stuck where we are, due to fate and economic whims completely beyond our control.

It has nothing to do with our "abilities!"

And excuse me while I punch you in the face.

8. So, those autopilots pretty much fly themselves, right?

So, your Cruise Control is pretty much your Designated Driver?

Autopilots are extremely sophisticated. They can fly from here to TOM (Timbuktu) with uncanny precision. Yep, just like a robot vacuum cleaner, which you can program to traverse every inch of your carpet . . . but don't dare move the furniture!

Autopilots are nothing more than a 3D cruise control. They can *process*, but they can't *think*.

For more, see my blog post, *"Busted Aviation Myths: Otto is My Copilot"*

7. Oh, you fly for Brand X? I flew them once. (Insert *Flight From Hell* tale of woe.) I'll never fly them again!

Gee, lemme break out my mini-violin.

Yes, yes, we all have our sob Flight From Hell stories. And, for airline crews, I'm convinced we're all required to have one at least every 6 months to remain "current and qualified."

Every airline in history has had their bad moments, but many of the factors are completely beyond their control: the weather, random mechanical, delay on a previous flight, etc.

In case you didn't know, with a million parts per bird, even the most stellar of machines break from time to time.

OK, so some airlines have worse reps than others, sometimes deservedly so. But please don't whine to us about it. We have no control over it, and the implication is that, since we're associated with that airline, we must suck, too.

If you really suffer that much on our airline getting from EWR to SFO, you can always go back to covered wagons.

And excuse me while I punch you in the face.

6. Is this thing safe?

If it wasn't, none of us would be here, the airline would be out of business, and there wouldn't even be an airline industry.

Moreover, people seem to forget the Number One Reason "this thing is safe": it's MY butt driving the pressurized metal tube hurtling at Mach .8— you think I'm gonna risk my tushy?

6.1 Corollary: "This plane's so small!" (Said while boarding anything not a Boeing 747, 777 or A380)

Yeah, lady, machines the size of cruise ships tend to have a little trouble on the takeoff roll.

And excuse me while I—*uh, ahem*. Welcome aboard!

5. (Said to the Flight Deck): Just so you know, I'm a Private Pilot, and I'm in back in case you need anything.

Uh, yeah, if we need to know the Vfe speed of a Cessna 172, we'll make an emergency PA for ya!

Most times #5 is said with a wink and we all just laugh, trade handshakes and welcome you aboard. But you can't believe how often said Private Pilot announces it with a serious, straight face.

Don't get me wrong, we all have 100% respect for the incredible accomplishment of achieving any pilot's license. But this statement sounds kind of like a 1st-year Medical student telling a heart surgeon he's available to take over. Or like punkass Wesley lecturing Cap'n Picard on the nuances of the Jeffries Tube Warp Drive plasma conduit—well, ok, that could happen, but you catch my drift.

4. Have you been drinking?

Just like the statement at a TSA checkpoint, "What, you think I have a bomb in my suitcase?" this one is just . . .

"PLANE" STUPID.

Believe it or not, morons have actually said this to crews as they approach the gate.

Result: the pilots stop everything to demand a pee pee test, and the flight is delayed for hours. And of course the offending passenger, if he knows what's good for him, slinks off to catch another flight before being lynched by his fellow seat mates.

Corollary: 4.1 Sorry, no crew discount.
Say what, Bartender?
OK, we are human, and some of us do occasionally drink on overnights to wind down. But we are EXTREMELY aware of our safe and legal limits, and of our report time the next day. We know that the most minor slip up would destroy our career.
So, bartender, pour me a double—and no tip for you!

3. You're too young to be a Pilot!

You got me, Ma'am. I'm really a burger flipper at McD's, and the airline is playing a cruel joke on you.

This implied insult negates the years of training and thousands of hours of flying your pilot no doubt already has under his/her belt.

Whether 3 stripes or 4 on those shoulder boards, rest assured they earned every one.

I used this line as a standing joke that burdens the main characters DC and Allen in *The Last Bush Pilots*. I've never actually heard it, but for 35 years I've read it in the horrified faces of my passengers—and I still do! For some reason, the traveling public expects all pilots to be elderly grandpas, born in the crib with 20,000 hours of flight time. Knock on wood, my silver hair still hides behind the blondish ones, all cut short to accent my perpetual Baby Face!

3.1 Corollary: You're a girl—girls don't fly!
Believe it or not, there's still moronic, backwoods, uneducated Neanderthals (feel free to add more insulting epithets) out there who still believe this.
Welcome to the 21st Century, pal!
You don't like it, feel free to crawl back into the cave from which you came. By the way: two of the best pilots I've ever known were—*gasp*—female!

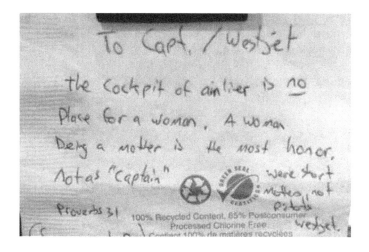

2. I'm Pregnant.

OK, I just had to throw that one in there for kicks. But, to answer the question that I KNOW is ever-looming in your dirty little mind . . .

NO, pilots and flight attendants are NOT running around sleeping with each other. Just like the environment at the office, however, they do work closely together, we're all human and the opportunity is there, so it does occasionally happen. Just not nearly as much as Hollywood or the gossiping busybodies would have you think.

1. You're a Pilot? Wow, you must be Rich!

Without elaborating too much on this subject, all I can say is that the vast majority of pilots spend tens of thousands of dollars on their aviation education, for the smallest chance of landing an airline job.

They will most likely work for years or even decades at food stamp wages to get there—and they may never get there.

And excuse me while I punch you in the face.

Honorable Mention: "Go Around! . . . Just kidding."

You probably heard this one in the news last year. Yep, it actually happened!

A very experienced ATL Tower controller, apparently bored with the graveyard shift, jokingly told Delta to go-around—that is, abort the landing, climb out and circle. A few seconds later, he added, "Just kidding." But it was too late. Delta, dutifully and correctly, instantly aborted and did a go-around—costing the Company who knows how many 100's of $ in fuel costs and inconveniencing passengers for another 15 minutes.

Go-arounds are common maneuvers, but they are no laughing matter. When a controller says, Go around!, you don't question it, you do it. You may initially have no idea why you're going around—a truck on the runway, a NORDO (no-radio) plane heading your way, who knows.

So, you shoot first and ask questions later.

Despite the typical melodrama the TV News Talking Heads spew about this sort of thing, however, there was absolutely NO risk to passengers during this very routine—if costly—maneuver.

We did a poll on Capn Aux Facebook page (facebook.com/CapnAux)

By a margin of 2-1, you voted to let the controller keep his job—after a little trip to the spankin' machine. I expect Delta will be sending him a fuel bill as well. I highly doubt the attached note will end with, "Just kidding."

Top Things to Never Tweet to a Pilot
Some funny ones sent in by YOU!

@BabyGorilla143: "Delta 214 go around……. Just kidding…"
(Added as an Honorable Mention, above!)

@Judge613: Hi, Jack!

@CaptJCKidder: We are from the FAA and we're here to help you! (One of the longest-standing jokes in the industry!)

@AZAviator: Can you put the instructor on the radio, please? (said to the instructor!)

@AirlineFlyer: Are we there yet?

@ShawnChittle: "So, where ya think that missing Malaysian plane is?"

@SmurfPilot: Maybe you're that way because you're not getting enough oxygen way up there.

@FlightChops (youtube.com/user/FlightChops): Know-it-all friend says, "Why do you study so much to fly on instruments? it's easy; I do it in *Flightsim* all the time!" (facepalm!)

@ComeBackDaddy (comebackdaddy.blogspot.com): Where's Baggage Claim? (Said while standing beneath the giant arrow pointing to Baggage Claim.)

Corollary: "Where's Flight 386?" (Said while standing beneath the gate info monitor. Lady, the only way I'd know off the top of my head where 386 was, is if I'm drivin' it!)

@JR_justJR (paxview.wordpress.com): When does this flight stop at the SkyMall? I really wanna do some shopping."

@Jayson_David Where did you get your wings; from a Cracker Jacks box? …(at FL 390) gonna open the door; stuffy in here ;D

@Millenia: "Are you the Pilot?" I always answer with: 1. Are you the passenger? 2. No, but I play one on TV! Or 3. No, but I stayed at a Holiday Inn Express last night!

(Multiple Tweeters):
Private Pilot says to the Captain:
"Hey, I think I could give you some landing tips;"
"Why didn't you do a proper run-up?";
"There's a funny noise over-wing. I've never heard it before."
"You know, your flaps were down for takeoff."
Etc. etc. etc., ad nauseum . . .

So, You Want to be an Airline Pilot?

Cap'n Dillon, a born pilot!
Photo courtesy Mom and Dad Haynes

I wrote this in response to the sheer volume of questions I was receiving via the blog (capnaux.com), email (eric@capnaux.com), even Twitter (@capnaux) and Facebook (facebook.com/CapnAux).

I would literally be asked the same battery of questions several times a day. Of course, I would always try to answer best I could and at length, but the task understandably became quite daunting.

After awhile, I noticed a pattern. Kids, young and old, were asking the same basic questions. "What college should I go to?" "Is this flight academy better than that?" "Where do I get money for training?"

In short, all their burning questions could be summed up in one:

"How do I become an airline pilot?"

So, I answered, best I could, once and for all.
No surprise, this became one of the most popular blog posts of 2014.

Ladies and gentlemen, from the flight blog, this is your Cap'n speaking. I have turned off the "Looming Pilot Shortage" sign (which has been on for 30 years now), and you are now free to pursue your aviation dream!

Honestly, for you up-n-comers, not since the Golden Age of Air Travel (circa 1950's) has there been such a pressing need for airline pilots!

The shortage, I believe, is no longer "Looming," but here. In the next 5-10 years, airlines—starting with the Regionals—are about to be caught with their blue uniform pants down. In fact, it's already happening.

"Yippee!" you shout, leaping for the sky. But then you land, and reality hits. So you ask, "Umm…how do I get there?"

Well, that's the multimillion dollar question, my friend, one that oodles and oodles of you have been asking me for the past three years! And I think it's high time I answered all of you.

First of all, some caveats:

- This is my *personal* take on matters, and I could easily be wrong.
- I started flying 35 years ago, and in this business, things change. I am completely unfamiliar, for example, with the whole new concept of "Flight Academies." Then again, many other things stay the same, such as some of the traditional roads to the airline cockpit.
- Speaking of changes, my advice below is subject to change by any number of factors. This is an extremely volatile business; the first to suffer in an economic downturn, and the last to recover. That "looming pilot shortage" may easily evaporate overnight due to economics, politics, terrorism, massive meteor impact … who knows what.
- I can only offer you *general* advice, and talk from my own, personal experience.
- As Confucius say, "I cannot lead you down the road; I can only point the way." *Each one of you* must seek and forge your own path to your dream job. And some of you WON'T make it. I'm not being pessimistic here, just realistic.
- I can *never* tell you "this college/flight school/path is better than that." If I did, I would be doing you a disservice, and would inevitably be wrong.
- Along the same lines, I can throw out some time-building suggestions, but it's up to you to figure out what works best for YOU.
- Finally, before you sink your life savings into this profession, read my post, *Top 10 Downers of an Airline Career*. (See my capnaux.com blog or *There I Wuz! Volume 1*.)

Still with me? OK, here goes …

THE AIRLINE COCKPIT IN 7 "SIMPLE" STEPS

STEP 1: GET GOOD GRADES!
Don't have 'em? Start NOW!

What? You're only in Kindergarten? Great! Get in the habit of getting A's. And, while you're at it, take advanced classes in, well, everything!

STEP 2: KEEP YOUR NOSE CLEAN!
A single DUI, marijuana charge or the mildest misdemeanor conviction could ban you from the airlines. Despite the "looming pilot shortage," there's still too many perfect pilots with perfect records out there.

STEP 2.5: Speaking of Which . . .

If you already have a pilot's license or two: don't get violated! Also, if you are worried at all about any medical conditions, spend $100 and get yourself a First Class Aviation Medical checkup. This will tell you if you'll even qualify—medically—for a pilot's license. For some conditions, there may be exemptions for which you can apply via the SODA program—of Demonstrated Ability. (By the way, your CPL will require vision correctible to 20/20, and no colorblindness.)

STEP 3: CIVILIAN OR MILITARY?
I know nothing about the military option, so if you choose it, you're on your own. Good luck, we're all counting on you—and your country is grateful for your service!

If you go civilian, you'll have to find a way to pay for all your training. If you can't afford it (or get amazing scholarships), then perhaps it's military for you. But, while your recruiter may promise you the moon—and an F-something strapped to your butt—you may find yourself committed to six years of deck swabbing.

Alternate Option: Go non-pilot military, get out asap, and use your GI bill to fund your civilian flight training. I know several who have gone or are going this route.

STEP 4 & 5: GO TO COLLEGE and/or START FLYING
You'll need to get:

1.) A 4-year degree (or 2-year at minimum).

2.) All your flight ratings.

By that, I mean through PPL (Private Pilot License), CPL (Commercial) and Instrument. You'll eventually need a Multiengine endorsement, and most likely also a CFI (Certified Flight Instructor.) When you get to 1,500 hours, you can finally get that Black Belt of pilot licenses, the ATPL (Airline Transport Pilot.)

You can do 1, then 2, or 2 then 1, or 1 and 2 together. Whatever works into your schedule and budget.

I started my PPL while in high school. Upon graduation, I enrolled in a junior college that specialized in flight training. In 2.5 years, I received all my basic flight ratings (CPL, Instrument, Multi, and CFI), along with a 2-year degree. Then I spent the next several years flight instructing while finishing up a 4-year degree.

STEP 6: BUILD FLIGHT TIME
Now comes the hard—and fun—part.

This is the "Catch-22" of aviation: How does a new pilot get a flying job without the flight time, and get the time without the job?

Just like DC and Allen in *The Last Bush Pilots*, this dilemma plagues every pilot at every stage of their career.

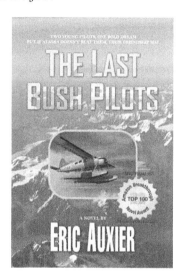

The most common entry-level job in flying is CFI (Certified Flight Instructor.)

I recommend starting out this way for 2 reasons: 1.) It's the easiest way to get a flying job or start your own business. 2.) By teaching others, you will *really* learn how to fly! You'll watch others make mistakes, and have to correct them. Many things you were fuzzy about will become clear.

Other possibilities: Banner Tow; sky dive hauler; crop duster (a dying breed); charter pilot; pipeline patrol; freight dog...the options are, well, not endless, but by the time you get to this point, you should have a good handle on what you will be able to do.

After you build several hundred—er, make that thousand, hours, you can advance to . . .

STEP 7: GET HIRED BY A REGIONAL . . . THEN A MAJOR
Because you've kept your nose clean, networked, kissed the appropriate butts, logged some stellar flight time, applied to every airline in the universe . . . you've managed to bag an interview!

You will FAIL.

Yes, that first interview is pretty much a given bomber. But keep plugging away! That first one was a great watershed test for you! You learned a ton. You'll have a fighting chance at the next one. The third, better than even odds. The fourth . . . you're in!

Then you'll be rolling in dough!

Eh, well, not exactly. (Now go back and read that *Top 10 Downers* post I was talking about!)

Cap'n Aux's Pilot Paycheck, Circa 80's-90's

ALMOST AWESOME
ALMOST DECENT
SO-SO
FOOD STAMPS
POOR HOUSE
MOM & DAD—HELP!

85   90

Frequently Asked Questions

• *What's the most common way to get to the airlines, civilian or military?*

Early on, it was military or nothing. Now, I believe, the pendulum's swung, with about 60% or more now coming from civilian ranks.

• *What's the best school or flight academy to go to?*

Again, I can't recommend specifics. Nor would I want to. The list is always changing, and only you can determine what fit is best for you. All that matters is that you: 1.) Have a 4-year degree; 2.) Have all your flight ratings, at least through instrument/CPL

• *Do you recommend ERAU (Embry Riddle Aeronautical University)? Do you recommend (your choice of institution here).*

I say again, I can't recommend specifics!

All I can say is, Embry Riddle DOES have a very good reputation…but it is about the most expensive club around, sort of the "Harvard" of aviation. Can you afford it? Only you can answer that.

Again, I *say again*: in the end, you need two things: 1.) All your flight ratings; 2.) A 4-year degree.

How you get them doesn't really matter!

• *What* ab initio *flight academy do you recommend? I want to bypass that 1,500 hour rule for the ATPL and get it at 1,000.*

What am I, a broken record? Again, I can't recommend anyone; I DON'T KNOW! Moreover, like I said above, it hardly will make a difference. I really am unfamiliar with the whole "flight academy" concept, so you're on your own with that. It does seem to be "the way of the future," however. Just make sure you're not spending more $$$ than you need to get the same thing.

One thing I will say about "ab initio" schools like ERAU, North Dakota, etc., is that they are able to get you both a 4-year degree and the ratings. Moreover, they are allowed to reduce the 1,500 hour ATPL requirement by 500 hours! But you have to do the math and figure out if that extra 500 is worth the extra expense of an academy like these.

• *That new FAA law requiring 1,500 hours for the ATPL (Airline Transport Pilot License) SUCKS! How do I deal with it?*

Well, ya, I agree. I think it's a political, knee-jerk, stupid, reactionary move. They raised the bar for no reason other than to look good to the ignorant public. However . . . IT HARDLY MAKES A DIFF.

You will probably need more than 1,500 hours to be attractive to a regional carrier—let alone a major—where an ATPL would be required. When I got hired by my 1st regional, I had about 3,000 hours; major: 5,500!

• *How do I make enough money for flying? How much do I need?*

That's the $100,000 question all of us have to figure out on our own! Get an inheritance! Get good grades and get scholarships! Sell your home and/or first born! And here's a concept: Work for it!

I'll mention again here the option of enlisting in the military, then once you get out, using your GI Bill to fund your training.

One bit of advice: if possible, instead of paying for an hour of training here and there only, when your paycheck allows it, save up a chunk of money FIRST then do it all at once. Otherwise, you'll be spending extra time and money just reviewing what you learned two months ago. But, if that's what you gotta do, that's what you gotta do. Again, everyone's situation is different.

• *What can I do right now if I'm too young (or can't yet afford) to start flight training or college?*

I like your attitude—you're being proactive!

Aside from getting stellar grades, go get a job at your local airport. Doing what? Anything, from cleaning toilets to fueling trucks! The point is to *network*—get your name and face out there, meet pilots, hear their stories, get to know them. When the time comes, you may have some great contacts to finagle free or cheap flight hours, trade menial jobs for flight time, etc. And when you do receive all your ratings, you may even have your first job lined up from your contacts!

• *C'mon, the Looming Pilot Shortage is here! Do I REALLY need a 4-year degree? Do I REALLY need good grades?*

YES! There's still a HUGE pool of qualified pilots out there, and for the foreseeable future, you need to be ultra-competetive. This may change over time, but for now, those just starting out...you need the whole shebang!

• *What should I fly, pistons, turboprops or jets?*

You'll fly whatever you can get your hands on and like it! (You really will!)

- *I'm gonna fly for (insert your favorite brand name here) Airlines cuz they're awesome!*

Hahahaha, you're so *cuuuute!*

You will fly for whomever the hell hires you, and LIKE IT!

That said, I did make it to my "dream" airline, by sending them one résumé a month for 5 years! But then the name on the door changed . . . then changed again . . .

Yep, your favorite brand may very well disappear in a merger, bankruptcy, etc. Remember Pan Am, TWA, and Eastern?

The name on the airline's door that hires you is no guarantee of the name that you retire from!

- *What type rating should I buy, B737 or A320?*

None of the above!

DON'T WASTE YOUR MONEY ON A TYPE RATING!!!

Anyone trying to tell you otherwise is trying to rip you off! It's like spending $10,000 on an advanced course in open heart surgery when you're a second year medical student. The only thing a type rating will do for a pilot with 1500 hours or less is provide a laugh for the people reading your résumé!

Once you start flying for an airline and rack up thousands of hours, THEN perhaps a type will be necessary. Southwest Airlines, for example, requires a B737 type before interview . . . *and* over 1,000 hours PIC (Pilot in Command) in a jet or turboprop.

There was ONE TIME in my life that I "bought" a type rating: *after* I had been hired and flew for a major airline. I was later furloughed (laid off). By then, I had about 7,000 hours of flight time and well over 1,000 hours PIC. A small airline was hiring, but a 737 type rating was required to apply. I blew $8,000 on a B-737 type. It seemed like a reasonable thing to do at the time . . . but I still didn't get the job.

That doesn't mean I wasted my money; it was a calculated risk that didn't pan out. But my point is, by the time I bought the type, I *was* qualified, and it could have possibly helped at that point. But a pilot with 400 hours and a 737 type (*sorry, nothin' personal*) would be laughed at!

The Most Important Career Advice I Can Ever Give You

You have chosen a potentially brutal, volatile, extremely stressful career. You have also chosen the greatest job that was ever conceived! There are absolutely NO guarantees that you will "make it." If you won't be happy until you land in the left seat of a jumbo jet, then . . . *stay out of this business!*

Pilots are typically goal-oriented people. They won't stop until the task is accomplished. This drive and focus will help you achieve your goal, but . . .

—Savor each and every moment of the journey!

—Never forget, from the first moment you step into that beat up old single engine Cessna for your very first flight lesson . . .

YOU ARE *ALREADY* LIVING YOUR DREAM!

Life is an adventure—and this career, exponentially so . . .

ENJOY THE RIDE!

SECTION 6: Love, Laughs . . . & Tears in the Sky

Photo of Cap'n Dillon; Pilot: Ed Duckworth

Cap'n Aux's Shattered Aviation Dream

This piece dedicated to the memory of Leslie Nielsen.
So long, and thanks for all the laughs!

This is a somewhat whimsical post I wrote early on for the blog, but I have to confess: it's truer than you think!

I've actually talked to pilots who had the venerable Leslie Nielsen aboard their ship, and apparently he did this very thing on every single flight. What a way to leave one helluvan aviation legacy!

For most pilots struggling up the aviation ladder, their singular focus is on their loftiest dream: to become an airline Captain. To have a fighting chance of getting there, they must endure years of food stamp wages, of studio apartment "crash pads" shared with six other similar pilot-dreamers; of Top Ramen meals, washed down with Pabst Blue Ribbon—just like college—but for six, or ten, or a dozen or more years. They must endure 6 on/1 off days of 8-leg, 16-hour, back-side-of-the-clock shifts, in earsplitting pistons, freighters, or turboprops.

I know I did. All for the ultimate dream of, one day, maybe, just maybe, having a shot at flying for a major airline.

And, God willing, if you actually got hired by a major, and that company actually stayed in business long enough...*mayhaps* you could even make it to the fabled Left Seat.

The standing joke in the cockpit is, You're not a real pilot till you've been divorced, furloughed, merged and through a Chapter 11 bankruptcy.

I'm a real pilot. Twice over. Two divorces, two furloughs, two mergers, three Chapter 11's, and even one Chapter 7—doors closed for good...

Looking back, however, I know I was more lucky than good. And *that*, ladies and gentlemen, is aviation's *real* "Right Stuff." Oh, yes, you need perseverance, determination, focus. And money, don't forget. Lots and lots of money, thrown at a dream that will most likely fail. But, above all, it takes pure luck.

Ultimately, I was one of the lucky few.

And yet, ironically, the Left Seat has never been my ultimate aviation dream.

No.

I dared to dream higher.

Much higher.

What, you may ask, could *possibly* be loftier than the left seat of a jet airliner?

Oh, you lowly mortals, with such pitiful, petty ambitions!

Many pilots, engineers and scientists were inspired by Neil Armstrong, Buzz Aldrin and the Apollo moonshots. Many NASA scientists and astronauts, in turn, often list *"Star Trek"* as their original inspiration. But for me, ever since the movie *"Airplane!"* debuted in 1980, I have known a singular purpose in life.

Sadly, however, on November 10, 2010, my dream was shattered.

I never did—and now never will—achieve my ultimate aviation dream. For, on November 10, 2010, the airline industry lost one of its most revered icons.

Leslie Nielsen, star of *"Airplane!"* died.

For, my life's dream has been this one thing: to have Leslie Nielsen poke his head into my cockpit before flight and announce, in pure, Lesliesque deadpan:

"I just wanted to tell you both, good luck. We're all counting on you."

Wiping away a single tear, I would have flown my flight. A perfect, error-free, baby's butt-smooth ride for my First Class passenger Mr. Nielsen.

I would have nailed a "roller" landing—my greatest ever—set the parking brake and walked off that plane, retired. Never to fly again.

And, dare I dream, a baggage cart would have run me over from behind, killing me instantly.

Fulfilled.

I know what you're saying: *Eric, surely you can't be serious!*
Yes I am serious.
And don't call me Shirley.

Leslie Nielsen and *Airplane!* Trivia:

-Leslie Nielsen was trained as an aerial gunner in WWII.

-His bio: en.wikipedia.org/wiki/Leslie_Nielsen

-Most of *Airplane!*'s jokes were based on the disaster movie, *Zero Hour*.

-*Don't call him Shirley. But you can call him Cap'n.* Early on in his career, Nielsen played no-nonsense Commander John J. Adams of the United Planets Cruiser C57-D in the 1965 movie, *Forbidden Planet*.

-To this day, over 35 years after its release, *Airplane!* is still quoted in cockpits around the world.

Roger. Over.

Dealing with Passengers— Don't Panic!

Photo by permission of shutterstock.com

This post bagged me one of my first "15 minutes of fame": I was quoted by the BBC! (Although, bless their hearts, they misquoted!)

A comical look at the quirky business of inflight passenger service, this post (and the ensuing 4-part series) nevertheless addresses some important concerns regarding passengers that the airline pilot must keep in mind.

"This is an emergency announcement," the female voice calmly declared in prim 'n proper English accent over the PA of the British Airways' 747—while cruising at 35,000 feet over the North Sea. *"We may shortly need to make an emergency landing on water."*

Minor detail: this "emergency announcement" was an *accidentally*-triggered prerecorded message. . . *accidentally* triggering 330 passengers to panic.

This embarrassing debacle reminds me of the old Airbus pilots' joke: "Ladies and gentlemen, we are flying a state-of-the-art, fully automated Airbus and nothing can go wrong *click!* go wrong *click!* go wrong . . ."

While I've have never had to deal with trying to calm down hundreds of panicked passengers inflight, there is definitely an acquired art to the making of a passenger PA.

Typically, flight attendants must read their briefings verbatim, but the pilots up front have much freer reign. Oh, sure we're required to grovel a bit to you and say, "Thank you for flying Very Fast airways. Buckle in, there is no need to panic," etc. But how we say it is largely left to us.

While I'm always tempted to simply say, "Welcome aboard, sit down, shut up, behave," and be done with it, that particular PA only works to cut the tension on the annual simulator check ride.

At least for me...

Rule # 1: the traveling public wants to be reassured.   They want their Captain to have a deep, gruff, authoritative but soothing *fatherly* voice, like George Clooney with a Texas drawl.

Unfortunately, my voice has been going through puberty for the past 35 years; I sound more like Cap'n Doogie Howser. Once, during a particularly early morning departure when my vocal chords were at their most relaxed, I thought I'd made the most manly PA of my life. But that fantasy was quickly shattered when two college kids poked their heads into the cockpit after the flight and said, "We just wanted to see who was flying, 'cause you sounded like you were 18!"

Since then, I've been resigned to my fate.

Rule #2: Humor is allowed over the PA, but you'd damn well better be good at it. If not, refer to Rule #1. While my buddy Captain Tony can keep his cabin in stitches for hours (*see endnote*), I found out a long time ago I'm in the "*Not* funny" category.

Once, on April Fool's Day, I diligently kept our passengers informed of our imminent arrival into RNO . . . during our flight to LAX. From the first announcement on, the flight attendants plagued the cockpit with pleas to correct the destination . . . the passengers were on the verge of mutiny! It was then that I learned: the pilot's voice over the PA is the Voice of God.

The age old turbulence/seat belt sign bit is an art unto itself as well. It boils down to this: one man's gentle rocking, nappy-time turbulence is another's "my God, my God we're all going to die!" . . . it's simply a matter of opinion. And the forecast of turbulence is just that: a prediction. Personally, I use the *SWAG* method: the "Scientific, Wild-A$$ Guess." Oh, sure, we can guesstimate by reading the clouds, listening to other aircraft's reports, etc. But in reality, there's no telling just what Mommy Nature has up her sleeve. In fact, it's so random, that we call the Seat Belt switch the Turbulence button: turn it off, get instant bumps. So, we try to err on the side of caution. In the end, really, the seat belt sign is nothing more than a Liability Switch: if it's on, get up at your own peril.

(BBC Quote alert! A portion of the following paragraph was used in an article entitled, "What Pilots' Won't Tell You!")

There is also an art to revealing just what's going on without giving away TMI. While I can't exactly jump on the PA and say, "Folks, pay no attention to the burning wing," I also must avoid describing *ad nauseum* exactly what the mechanics onboard are fixing. For example, I can't launch into a five minute dissertation of just why our our IAE V-2533-A5 Engine Number 2's ECU (Engine Control Unit) on the FADEC (Full Authority Digital Electronic Control) is triggering spurious warnings from the SDAC (System Data Acquisition Concentrator) to the EWC (Engine/Warning Display) without sounding alarmist. And I certainly can't say, "The *doohicky* on the *whatchamajig* is causing quite a nasty ruckus with that *gizmo* thingy." But I can say, "Our ace mechanics are onboard resetting one of our black boxes. We should be under way in a few minutes."

Bottom line: Trust us. It's OUR butts in the plane, too, and we ain't gonna risk it, PERIOD!

— — —

Cap'n Aux, in the middle of one of his exceptional—if rather non-humorous—PA's . . . But he still sounds—and looks—like Cap'n Doogie!

— — —

*Example of classic Tony PA: "Attention K-Mart shoppers, we have a blue light special on aisle . . . oh, sorry, that's my day job. Ahem! *(deep, gruff George Clooney voice with a tinge of Texas drawl)* This is your Captain speaking . . ."

Dealing with Passengers Redux—Make My Day!

I have a Napoleon Complex: I am spring loaded to kick your obnoxious arse off my plane. My motto is, "Welcome Aboard! Make My Day." About the only thing holding me back is having to do the required paperwork.

9/11 did one good thing: it put "Command Authority" back in the hands of *El Cap-i-tan*. Moreover, when necessary, an airport full of bored cops eagerly awaits our phone call.

Of course, I must have sound reason for my actions. Obviously, "Safety" is always the bottom line. Some other clearly-crossed lines are: drunk and/or disorderly, smokin' in the boys' room, failure to obey a crew member, and physical or verbal abuse.

On the other side of the line, the *Disabilities Act* forbids me from passenger removal for disabilities resulting in the "appearance or involuntary behavior that would annoy or inconvenience others." Moreover—sadly—I *cannot* eject you for your horrid body odor.

In between those lines, however, there's about 50 shades of grey.

"Suspicious behavior"…hmm, where's that line?

For me, it boils down to, "are you comfortable transporting this passenger?" Or, "will it interfere with your duties?" One thing I've learned these past 35 years in the sky: a problem on the ground nearly always becomes a bigger problem upstairs.

Another thing I must keep in mind are the passengers around the weirdo. As mentioned in my article, "Terror in the Skies!", post-9/11 passengers are spring-loaded to pounce on anyone behaving the slightest bit odd; they're my own personal, onboard SWAT team.

But what if the poor schmuck is simply on meds and can't help himself? Take that behavior up to altitude (8,000' of air pressure inside the cabin at cruise altitude), and those medical effects can amplify. Since I can't legally boot the weirdo off, we gotta keep a keen eye on the on-board SWAT team.

———

"Hello, ATC? This is Cap'n Aux. Send the TSA, FBI, CIA, SWAT, and Seal Team 6! Why? Oh, some guy wouldn't stop talking on his cell."

———

About once or twice a year I get to boot a drunk, smoker, or obnoxious moron off the ship. That's on average.

Once, I had to do it two flights in a row…

The first was a trio of young male passengers surreptitiously using walkie talkies to communicate in flight. A huge no-no, and one that actually interfered with our radios. At first we thought we had a "stuck microphone" on frequency, which squeals every time someone else transmits. But when we switched to a new ATC freq, we heard the same squeal.

FO Tom and I were just scratching our heads when the lead flight attendant called to report the disturbance. I ordered the FA's to confiscate their gear. But when confronted, each suspect claimed they had no such item —even though multiple passengers saw them.

Ah! No problem. Cap'n Napoleon knows how to deal with this. One simple radio call, and upon landing the suspects were personally welcomed to LAX by airport police officers, who escorted the gentlemen off the plane and into the loving hands of the FBI.

The second flight was much simpler.

Kicked a guy off for smokin' in the boys' room. No brainer. C ya! (The fact that he was a smelly guy on meds had nothing to do with it!)

Then there was that kid in KELP with a passel of razor blades spilling out of his backpack.

Um, TSA, hello?!

Needless to say, he spent an extra night in El Paso contemplating his travel packing techniques...

———

Sigh. A Cap'n Can Dream . . .

———

Even when a deranged wannabe hijacker does manage to sneak aboard and cause a ruckus, he is often easily thwarted by using his whackiness against him.

Once, long before 9/11, my former airline in the Caribbean had a hijack incident by just such a nut bag.

Just before landing at SJU, he burst into the cockpit and demanded to be flown to Cuba. The Captain said something like, "Yes, sir, right away, sir! But first we'll need to refuel."

After landing, the Captain advised the hijacker that he and the FO would have to walk over to the terminal and sign for it.

His answer was a brilliant, "Duh . . . okay!"

Of course, half of Puerto Rico's police force showed up before the fuel did. That poor sumbich didn't make it to Cuba either.

Similar stories in the news afford equally entertaining scenarios:

—Thou shalt not pose as a pilot and use fake id's to hitch a free ride aboard an airliner, a la the infamous "Catch Me if You Can" antihero Frank Abignale. Result: arrest on suspicion of endangering airline security and "usurping a title."

—Thou shalt not slap the passenger ahead of you for reclining his seat into your lap. Result: restraint in plastic cuffs and arrest upon landing.

—Thou shalt not call in a bogus terror threat accusing your love's new boyfriend on his plane flight. Result: Arrest by the FBI and charges carrying up to 10 years in prison.

—Thou shalt not wear a shirt on board a plane mocking the TSA and stating, "Bombs,ZOMG/ZOMG terrsts." Result: ejection from said plane.

—Thou shalt not lock oneself in the cockpit before flight to morn a recent breakup. Result: removal and arrest.

—Thou shalt not punch another passenger inflight, and yell profanities at other passengers and flight crew...even if you're just a drunken grandma. Result: Pilot turns plane around and lands, and naughty, wasted grannie removed and arrested, to sobered off in the slammer.

My Pilot Hero: Captain Mary Grace Baloyo

The following is a Historical narrative. This is a true story, as close as the facts will allow. But, where there are blanks in the data, I speculate on what exactly happened in the cockpit, and what could have been going through our heroine's head at the moment.

I dare you to read this with dry eyes. I know I can't.

Courage is the price that Life exacts for granting peace,
The soul that knows it not, knows no release
from little things.
—Amelia Earhart

You have not heard of Philippines Air Force pilot Mary Grace Baloyo.

She did not set foot on the moon. She did not break the sound barrier, design a game-changing jet engine or make the Smithsonian Air & Space museum.

But, as you shall see, she fully deserves our recognition, praise and gratitude.

Indeed, Grace was awarded—posthumously—Philippine's highest military award: The Medal of Valor.

She is one of only four recipients.

But, while she received many combat medals, she did not win this one in battle . . .

Clark Air Base, Philippines

The day dawned hot, sticky and rainy on March 26, 2001 at Atienza Air Base in Sangley Point, Pampanga, Philippines, home of the PAF 15th Strike Wing. The base was named after war hero Major Danilo Atienza, a PAF pilot who, during a 1989 coup attempt, crashed and was killed on this very base.

And it is an honor to follow in his footsteps, thought 27-year-old Captain Grace Baloyo, as she preflighted her OV-10 Bronco close air support aircraft.

Little did she know how literally she would follow in his footsteps.

Grace was not a Captain yet. She was a 1st Lieutenant in the Philippines Air Force. She would be awarded the lofty title of Captain posthumously, after this day, after this flight—the last of her life.

Today's mission: a proficiency checkride and bombing exercise over Crow Valley gunnery range with her "copilot," Air Force training Captain Ben Nasayao, and 2 other Broncos in formation, laden with inert bombs.

Removing the protective cover and peering down the intake duct, Lt. Grace inhaled the pungent odor of hydraulic fluid and burnt oil. The sound of military strike engines spooling up around her sent a shock wave of excitement buzzing up her spine.

The distinct combination of senses took her back to her earlier training days and combat missions.

In 1995, she'd joined the Philippine Air Force as an aviation cadet.

How young and naive I was! she thought with a chuckle.

Having aced all the required military courses and rigid training regimens, she later became one of only six female combat-qualified pilots of the PAF.

As she watched a U.S. F-18 taxi by her, Grace reflected on her active military life.

She'd seen combat action as an attack and bomber pilot in the many military operations against the Moro Islamic Liberation Front and communist insurgencies in Mindanao, the Visayas and Luzon.

But being the most decorated female pilot in the PAF didn't go to her head. To be sure, she knew, the 8 Gold & 1 Bronze Crosses, 2 Distinguished Aviation Crosses, and 4 Military Merit Medals for heroism and gallantry in action had been an honor to receive.

But not even the Golden Eagle Merit Medallion given to me by President Gloria Arroyo herself can beat the pungent smell of hydraulic fluid and burnt oil on a hot, rainy day in the Philippines, she thought.

To Lt. Grace, the sounds, sights, and odors tasted of . . . *adventure.*

She pushed to the back of her head the added excitement of her pending December marriage to her fiancee, Air Force 1Lt. Ditto Nestor Dinopol.

She completed the aircraft inspection and hopped in.

Despite fighting through turbulence and heavy rain showers all morning, Lt. Grace performed a near-flawless checkride.

"Take us home," barked Captain Nassayao.

"Yes, sir!" replied Lt. Grace, banking smartly away from the gunnery range, a thin smile on her lips.

Tonight, Nestor, we celebrate.

The anniversary of their dating was only four days away . . .

Lt. Grace heard a loud *thunk!* followed by violent shaking. A glance outside: her left engine had disintegrated in a ball of fire. Kicking the autopilot off, she fought the suddenly sluggish stick.

Immediately, Captain and Lieutenant raced through the *Emergency Engine-Fire and Shutdown Checklist*:

"Power lever—idle!"

"Idle!"

"Engine kill switch—off!"

"Off!"

"Fire bottle—Discharged!"

"Discharged!"

But the engine still burned.

"Mayday, mayday," Lt. Grace called over the radio, "Bronco Six-Seven declaring an emergency! Number one engine fire. Request vectors to Clark International Airport."

"Bronco Six-Seven," replied the Tower, "turn right heading two-three-zero. Cleared to land Runway Two-Zero. Fire trucks are rolling."

As much as she dared, Lt. Grace banked the now violently-shaking plane toward the runway. Suddenly, she felt her guts lift.

They were dropping—fast.

"We're not going to make the field, Lieutenant!" shouted the Captain over the intercom.

She glanced below. Despite the torrential rain and near-zero visibility, she could see that they were directly over a residential subdivision in the town of Mabalacat, Pampanga province.

"We'll make it, Captain," Grace replied. "We—We have to."

"That's a negative, Lieutenant. *EJECT, EJECT, EJECT!*" ordered Captain Nasayao.

"But—"

Suddenly behind her, she heard the Captain blast out of the cockpit. The angry sky rushed in, a maddening cacophony of torrential rain and gale force wind.

She reached for the Eject handle, but hesitated. She looked down. The ground was rushing up fast—and with it, homes loaded with people. Hundreds of innocent people.

Biting her lip, she let go of the handle.

Lt. Grace disobeyed the order, the last one ever given to her by a superior officer of the PAF.

Instead, she banked hard right, fighting the protesting airplane.

The wild bucking Bronco screamed, cried, fought its lone rider with all its might.

But Lt. Grace remained in the saddle.

She used every muscle, every fiber, every precious moment and skill of her stellar Air Force training and combat experience to force the crippled machine to bend to her will.

Even so, she could not will it back into the air.

She firewalled the good engine, racing against time to escape the population center

The ground raced up.

Forgive me, Nestor. I won't be there tonight to celebrate with you. Nor will I make our wedding. I love you. Fare well.

"Let go, I've got you now," a new Voice spoke in her head.

This time, Lt. Grace obeyed her Superior Officer.

Suddenly filled with an inexplicable peace, Mary Grace Balayo let go of the burning craft and closed her eyes.

In a vacant lot, one block away from the nearest home, the Bronco exploded in flames.

Miraculously, the inert ordnance remained intact.

Lt. Grace alone perished, and in so doing, saved countless lives on the ground.

As befitting a hero who goes down with the ship, Lt. Grace was posthumously promoted to the rank of Captain.

For her "conspicuous gallantry and intrepidity at the risk of life above and beyond the call of duty," Captain Grace was also posthumously awarded the Medal of Valor.

Philippine President Gloria Arroyo personally handed the medal to Lt. Baloyo's parents, Romeo and Annie.

And with that, aviation history was made . . .

For Captain Mary Grace Baloyo became the first and only woman in Philippines history to received her country's highest military award for heroism.

"To fly West, my friend, is a flight we must all take for a final check."
—Author Unknown

This story borrows heavily from the excellent narrative at:
angelfire.com/ga/batwentyone/valor.html

SECTION 7: Novel Idea! Book Excerpts

The Last Bush Pilots
Winner—Amazon Top 100 Breakthrough Novels 2013!

Two young pilots. One bold dream.
But if Alaska doesn't beat them, their friendship may.

I wrote *The Last Bush Pilots* out of sheer awe.

Awe of a world as magnificent and alien to me as Planet Pandora.

The world: Alaska.

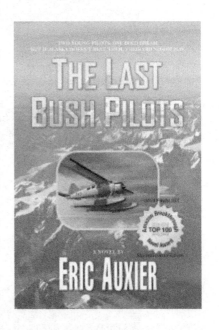

The Alaskan people—especially the pilots—were larger than life, and seemed to thrive in the harsh and indescribably lovely land that each one had fallen in love with. Indeed, I did, too.

I simply *had* to share with the world the magnificence that was Alaska.

Most of the characters in the novel were inspired by real-life personalities, and Jake "Crash" Whitakker is no exception.

In a way, each character represents an aspect the land itself, and Jake perhaps personifies the land better than any other: wild, untamed, magnificent in stature, and completely unpredictable.

Excerpt—Chapter 5: Jake "Crash" Whitakker

In the ego-filled world of Alaskan commercial pilots, Jake Whitakker was the undisputed king of flight. This was not consciously acknowledged by those around him, it was simply understood as fact. Many disagreed with his cowboy ways in the cockpit, especially FAA Inspector Bruner and his government cohorts back in Oklahoma City.

Nevertheless, Whitakker's airmanship remained unquestioned. And as a hunting and fishing guide, Jake Whitakker had no equal.

Born in Kalispell, he spent much of his youth hunting the Montana wilds under his prospector daddy's muddy boots. With Mom gone long before his memory, young Jake learned to bring home the buck and skin it while Dad panned and sluiced his way across the Rockies, Canada, and finally Alaska. Squandering a healthy family inheritance, father and son traveled in an aging Piper Super Cub, which Jake soloed before his thirteenth birthday.

A year later, his flight-of-fancy life suddenly crashed and burned.

In a bar room shootout over a shady lady, Jake lost his one anchor: his friend, his mentor, his hero. His dad. For the first time in his life, Jake was alone. Abandoned by the one he loved.

Devastated, a wall went up around him.

Authorities sent the wild boy to a Catholic orphanage. Though Catholic on the birth certificate, he'd rarely set foot in a church. Like Tarzan coming to the city, he didn't fit in, didn't belong. And he didn't care. Weekly fistfights with the other boys and the nuns' daily knuckle rappings did little to temper his demeanor, for the seeds of his life had already been sewn. Jake Whitakker was a renegade and mountain man, born and bred.

After high school, to finance his commercial flight training, he landed a summer job on a forest fire fighting crew. Each season he worked up the fireman's ladder, eventually landing in the copilot seat of a slurry bomber, a modified C-130. Flying troops and slurry over the burning brush, he and his crew squeezed the four-engine turboprop plane into and out of some of the shortest dirt strips in the country.

Once, during a low pass over a particularly hot fire, an underground fuel tank exploded, sending liquid fire and shrapnel flying into his path. He banked hard and climbed, but too late.

The number two engine disintegrated and his right wing caught fire. Before the captain and crew realized what had even happened, he calmly deadsticked the craft into a meadow, dumping the slurry as he did. The plane landed, wheels up, in a cloud of red dust. The fire retardant doused the flames, and though the plane was a total loss, the men escaped with few injuries and no burns.

The action earned him command of his own ship, and the dubious nickname of "Crash."

A small scar from that action graced his square chin cleft, complimenting his woodsman's good looks. And at six feet two of swaggering muscle, he was equally skilled at landing ladies.

During winter months he flew, backpacked and hunted the wilds of North America. His outdoor talents caught the eye of a U.S. Fish and Wildlife official, who talked him into taking on another role: Game Warden. Jake's contempt for poachers nearly equaled his passion for hunting, as only a man brought up firsthand to understand nature's delicate balance could. He added to the

Department's arsenal a most effective weapon: a floatplane. With great mobility, efficiency and zeal, the man enforced his beat.

It was an idyllic, if ironic, existence for the wild man. But even along the Canadian border, civilization hounded him. Finally, a tough young Yupik Eskimo named Sophie, working a summer job for the forest service, caught his eye. Sparks flew as hot as the embers from his old job, melting the glacial ice around his heart. But when the season ended, despite Jake's frantic pleading, she returned to her native village of Akiachak, Alaska.

Abandoned yet again by the one he loved, Jake was crushed. He took a long hard look at his life, then looked at her photo. He recalled his youth in the vast Alaskan Interior. The land and Sophie beckoned.

"To hell with it," he said, and followed her to Alaska.

The love affair, so perfect in the Lower Forty Eight, was a train wreck. Only Eluk, the family's new Alaskan Malamute puppy, seemed to enjoy his presence. Including Sophie.

Sensing her slipping away, he begged her to marry him. She refused. More to the point, her family refused. While a *Gussik* husband might mean a step up in wealth, a pilot would never be around to help during the tough times. Moreover, Sophie's father had other plans for her, in the form of a tribal official in Bethel.

Jake left with his tail between his legs. With his tail wagging, Eluk followed. Except for the affection Jake felt for his new companion, the glacial wall around his heart refroze. He fled as far as possible, to the opposite corner of the state, from Sophie. But never again did he leave Alaska.

Joining an upstart air taxi firm in Juneau called Southeast Alaskan Seaplanes, Whitakker quickly gained a reputation as one of the region's premier hunting and flying guides.

But that was not the only fame he gained. While some said he invited the worst of luck, to pilots he enjoyed the best. Starting with his legendary slurry bomber crash, Jake survived no less than two accidents and three "incidents," as the National Transportation Safety Board called his minor crackups in typically dry government legalese. He walked away from them all. And, while eighty percent of all aviation crashes were attributed, rightly or wrongly, to "pilot error," only one was ever blamed on him.

The accident had occurred in Gastineau Channel. Summer tourist season had brought yet another luxury cruise ship into port, and while some passengers power-shopped downtown, the more adventurous signed up for the SEAS' glacier "flightseeing" tours.

Sunny skies and whitecaps promised a scenic but bumpy ride for Whitakker's passengers.

A barf bagger day for sure, Jake thought with a grim smile, as he flew his floatplane up the Gastineau Channel toward the cruise ship.

Jake's de Havilland Beaver led a squadron of cohorts, strung in trail from the airport. Like Navy pilots in a carrier pattern, each planned to touch down, glide up to the ship dock, load up and launch again, only seconds apart. All part of the show.

Slowing the Beaver to final approach speed, Whitakker scanned the channel for boat and plane traffic. Calculating wind, waves and channel current, he selected the prime touch down point which would slide his bird up to the dock with minimal work.

Off to one side, an inebriated boatload of partiers raced along the channel. Beer goggles firmly in place, the speedster blasted through the waves, happily oblivious to anything as strange as an air ship landing on water. With a playful laugh, his woman poured a Budweiser over his head. In retaliation, he swerved to plop her back down in her seat. The action sent him straight for Whitakker.

Out of the corner of his eye, Jake caught the motion. The boat he'd dismissed as nonthreatening was now heading straight for him.

Whitakker banked sharply right. At the same moment, a wind gust stalled his lower wing, which dropped further, catching the tip in a wave. The plane cartwheeled and flipped.

Suddenly Whitakker found himself upside down, looking through the windscreen at the murky green depths of the channel. He gasped as freezing water poured in. Releasing his harness, Jake "fell" to the ceiling, his head hitting hard and submerging in water. He fumbled to slide the window open and the water gushed in. Finally, when enough water filled the cabin to equalize the pressure, he popped open the door and swam out.

Disoriented, he eyed the bubbles rising about him, and swam with them to the surface. Lungs nearly bursting, he broke surface. He gasped for air, twice sucking in seawater as the rough waves slapped at him. He dragged himself onto the nearest float, now floating upside down.

Shocked, the drunks circled to rescue him. They pulled up in time to see a figure standing on the float and looking like a humiliated, rain-soaked cat. As they eased up along side, Whitakker turned to them, a look of murder in his eyes.

Thinking twice about rescue, the driver shifted into reverse. "Uh, hey there, buddy," he said, "I'll go for help."

The drunk hit the throttles, but the cat leaped, landing on him with all his weight.

By the time the others pulled Whitakker off him, the driver sported a broken nose, two missing teeth, and a gouge above his left eye that took eighteen stitches to close.

Assault charges were never pressed, but the incident bought him a one-month pilot license suspension for *Careless and Reckless Operation of an aircraft.*

And one month's free drinks at the Red Dog Saloon.

CODE NAME: DODGER
Mission 1: Operation Rubber Soul

A Young Adult "Spy/Fly" Adventure Series

TEENER-SKATER-PUNKER - SPY

My name's Justin Reed, a fourteen-year-old New York street kid, orphaned when my dad was murdered by the evil spy Pharaoh.

CIA Case Officer Bob Cheney discovered the Pharaoh was after me, too, so he took me into protective custody.

The Artful Dodger was my code name, and Bob, code name Fagin, trained me in all sorts of cool spy stuff: advanced self-defense, weapons, surveillance, evasion and survival. "The Company" even taught me how to use some sneaky spy gadgets.

But I had other plans.

Escaping CIA custody, I used my old street smarts—and new CIA training—to track down the Pharaoh myself.

But, I quickly learned, I was no match for a seasoned killer.

"An all-time fun ride! Mr. Auxier hit a big win on this. Looking forward to the series!"

—Karlene Petitt, Airline Pilot-Author, *Flight for Success*

"I'm 50 years older than the target market for this book, and I couldn't put it down!"

—George Nolly, airline pilot-author, *Hamfist* trilogy

Mission 2: Cartel Kidnapping

The long-awaited sequel to Code Name: Dodger!

"Who is the great CIA Agent, Artful Dodger? Tell me now, and I kill you quick."

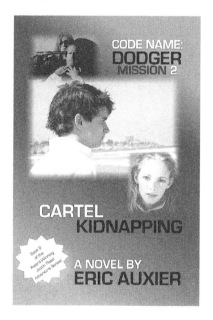

CIA Case Officer Bob Cheney is kidnapped, and teen orphan Justin Reed—aka the Artful Dodger—tracks his newly-adoped father to a top secret smuggling base, where he is forced to match wits with the cartel family's brilliant teen prodigy, Luis Ocho.

But Luis's stunning sister Kiara is another story. Is she falling for Justin, or is this just another one of Luis's diabolical tricks to lure the "great Agent Dodger" to his demise?

Once again, Justin is forced to rely on his old street smarts—and his new CIA training—to face a ruthless enemy.

A sequel to *Code Name: Dodger*, *Mission 2: Cartel Kidnapping* continues the adventures of teen orphan Justin Reed, and is a Young Adult, action adventure spy series for kids of all ages.

"Like Harry Potter, *this YA series is fun for kids of all ages!"*
  —Tawni Waters, author, *Beauty of the Broken*
"I didn't think it was possible to improve on the first book, but it happened !"
  —Octavious L., Florida

Coming Soon!

Mission 3: Jihadi Hijacking—Excerpt

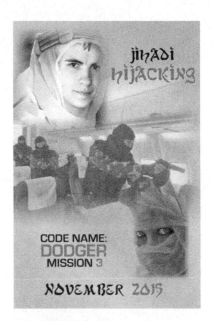

When their Airbus A321 is hijacked by armed terrorists at 30,000', it's up to Bob and Justin to take it back.

But that's only half the problem: once they overcome the terrorists, who's left to fly the plane?

Every passenger's nightmare . . .

And every Virtual Sim Pilot's fantasy!

CODE NAME:
DODGER
MISSION 3

ΝΟΥΣΜΒΣR 2015

Excerpt:

AGENCE INTERNATIONALE DE L'ANTI-TERRORISME

TOP SECRET—EYES ONLY—EXTREMELY URGENT
TO: KING COLE/ITA HQ
FM: MOSSAD
LOC: JERUSALEM, ISRAEL
RE: OPERATION SPEARHEAD
LOST CONTACT WITH EURECONO AIR FLT 924, A321 AIRLINER, ENRT TLV, DURING COVERT SURVEILLANCE OF TARGETS. SUSPECT HIJACKING.
AGENTS ABOARD: FAGIN/DODGER.
END MSG.

PROLOGUE

EurEcono Air Flight 924
Airbus A321
32,000′ MSL over the Mediterranean

It really wasn't my fault this time.

They were going to kill the guy, and I just wasn't going to let that happen.

The first hijacker wore a red headband with some sort of Arabic writing and held a Glock 38 pistol in his hand, making him look scary as all get out. He had it aimed at some random guy, who was cowering in his seat six rows ahead of us.

The terrorist scumbag was ready to pull the trigger.

* * *

We were just about to start down into Tel Aviv when it happened.

Since the plane was nearly empty, my adopted dad Bob and I had a row to ourselves in Coach. I had my nose pressed to the window, while Bob sat in an aisle seat, reading. He was combing through a stack of electronic pages on his laptop that all said something like, *Consolidated Industries, Inc.* on the letterhead. But I knew they were actually some of his insanely boring Top Secret intelligence briefs from his boss, ITA Director Allen Cole.

"Old King Cole," as we called him, was now Director of the U.S. branch of the brand new, *über* top-secret, *Agence internationale de l'anti-terrorisme*, which sounded pretty cool in French. But in English, was kinda lame: International Anti-Terrorism Agency, or ITA. In public, we simply called it, "the Business," just like we secretly called CIA, "the Company."

And Bob was Cole's right hand man. His title: "Deputy Director, Clandestine Operations"—espionage-ese for *Head Spy*.

Bob's new "legend," or permanent cover story, was that he still worked for the CIA. LMAO, what a cover! I still snickered that one.

See, as far as the public was concerned, the ATI didn't exist. From what I could figure, ATI infiltrated the bad guys with spies and hi tech stuff like drones and satellites, and then foiled their plots by unleashing their black ops troops—nicknamed Reapers—to, uh, *dispatch* them, quickly and quietly.

No politics, no red tape, no judge or jury. Just Reapers.

Unfortunately for us, there wasn't a single Reaper onboard.

Just the passengers, the crew . . .

And half a dozen seriously-armed hijackers.

First we heard a commotion up front, in First Class. Then, four dudes in our section jumped out of their seats, red headbands over their heads and shouting *Allah ackbar!* and such. Two were waving Glock handguns, the other two, knives. How they'd smuggled those aboard, I hadn't a clue.

People screamed. A flight attendant dropped her serving tray and fainted, right there in the aisle beside us.

Bob yanked her out of harm's way, just as a perp ran up the aisle to the front of our section.

"We are God's beloved soldiers of the World Islamic State," the man before us announced. "By His blessing, WIS has overcome the cockpit and are now in command of this vessel."

Around us, passengers gasped. Bob and I traded worried glances.

Strolling towards us, he continued. "Remain in your seats, and most of you will not be harmed."

"*Most?*" I whispered to Bob.

With his eyes, Bob directed me to look at his hands in his lap. With his fingers, he quickly "spoke" to me in American Sign.

It had been months since CIA Communications training, so I was a little rusty.

"Don't move a muscle," he signed. "It's a terror suspect and his cell. I didn't tell you this because it's Classified, but I'm assigned to monitor his movements. To discover his plans."

Gazing at him in pure disbelief, I signed back, "I guess we know his plans now."

I glanced behind us. Two terrorists paced up and down the single aisle in our section, eyeing the passengers.

I looked back at Bob. I signed, "We can take 'em."

Bob shot me an alarmed look. "Stand down, Dodger!" he signed back. "We're outgunned, outnumbered, and there may be Sleepers," he said, referring to more terrorists that might still be posing as passengers.

"Cooperate," the hijacker continued, "and all of you non-Zionists will live." He strolled down the aisle toward us, and stopped by a man wearing a Jewish *yamaka*. "If you do not believe me, then this will be your fate."

To my horror, he aimed his Glock at the side of the man's head.

So, despite Bob's strict orders to stay seated and shut up, I jumped out and ran up the aisle toward the terrorist.

"My God! My God! We're all gonna die!" I screamed, flailing my arms in the air like I was some kid spazzing out.

The slimeball snapped his head toward me.

Then his gun.

Release Date: November 5, 2015!
Books Link: amazon.com/author/ericauxier

AFTERWORD

Alas, we have come to the end of our adventure . . . for now.

I hope you've enjoyed Volume II! If you purchased this in print on Amazon, you can pick up the eBook version for just $1.99 through their Match program. The eBook includes color photos, videos and live links. And if you haven't read it yet, Volume I is available there as well!

I'll be back next year with Volume III. In the mean time, join me at capnaux.com, and watch for my articles in such publications as *Airways* Magazine, and online at AirwaysNews.com and NYCAviation.com.

Drop me a line any time at eric@capnaux.com.

More links to my stuff such as Twitter, Facebook, Instagram, vimeo, etc. are listed on the next page.

This is Cap'n Aux, signing off!

ABOUT THE COVER PHOTO

Photo by Mark Lawrence (see Bio opposite page)

Aircraft: Aer Lingus A330-301
Registration: EI-DUB
Name of Aircraft: St. Padraig
Departing runway 4L at JFK Airport on its return flight to Dublin.

Shot in RAW with a Nikon D50 w/Nikon 80-400 f/4.5-5.6D VR lens.
Focal length for the shot: 310mm. Aperture: F/5.3. Shutter speed:
1/320s, ISO 800.
Editing of the picture done with Adobe PhotoShop CC for Windows.

Visit Mr. Lawrence's photography Blog at: amateuravphoto.blogspot.com
See Mr. Lawrence's Portfolio at marklawrence.zenfolio.com

THE MEN BEHIND THE COVER

COVER PHOTO—MARK LAWRENCE

Also responsible for the magical cover photo from There I Wuz! Volume 1, photographer Mark Lawrence is an avgeek that has been around the industry since he was a small child.

An aviation photographer for many years, he is also the Producer for the aviation website NYCAviation.com. He makes his home in Fort Lauderdale, Florida with his wife and son. email: mark@tavustheman.com.

COVER DESIGN
GINO LUIS AVENTURERA

Gino Luis Aventurera is an artist and graphic designer.

He also collaborated with Eric Auxier on the cover of There I Wuz! Volume I as well as Mr. Auxier's novel, The Last Bush Pilots. He is a graduate student from Arizona State University and is currently residing in Phoenix, Arizona. email: ginoluis@hotmail.com

LINKS to All Things Cap'n Aux

AUTHOR'S BLOG

Adventures of Cap'n Aux: capnaux.com

The Last Bush Pilots & Other Works

Amazon Author Page: amazon.com/author/ericauxier

To explore more about *The Last Bush Pilots*: lastbushpilots.com

To order in Print: createspace.com/4053153

To order in eBook: goo.gl/NCvGuW

Book Trailer: vimeo.com/52958425

Mayday! Trailer: vimeo.com/capnaux/mayday

Code Name: Dodger Trailer: vimeo.com/capnaux/cnd

Cartel Kidnapping Trailer: vimeo.com/capnaux/cndodger2

Author Social Media

Facebook: facebook.com/CapnAux

Twitter: twitter.com/capnaux

Instagram: instagram.com/capnaux

Vimeo Page: vimeo.com/capnaux

Featured Video: *Cap'n Dillon's Ecstatic Adventure!*
    vimeo.com/capnaux/dillon

Other Links

Stories on AirwaysNews: airwaysnews.com/blog/?s=auxier

Stories on NYCAviation: nycaviation.com/author/eauxier/

Contact the Author

eric@capnaux.com

ABOUT THE AUTHOR

Eric "Cap'n Aux" Auxier is a pilot by day, writer by night, and kid by choice.

Never one to believe in working for a living, his past list of occupations include: Alaska bush pilot, freelance writer, mural artist, and pilot for a Caribbean seaplane operation. He is now a captain for a major U.S. airline.

Mr. Auxier has contributed to such worldwide publications as *Arizona Highways, Airways* Magazine, *Plane & Pilot* and *AOPA Pilot*. He is a graduate of Arizona State University (B.S. degree in Aeronautical Technology; minors in Journalism and Japanese) and Cochise College (A.S. degree in Pro-Pilot and Creative Writing). At both institutions, he worked as a newspaper editor, staff reporter and columnist.

There I Wuz! Volume II is his fifth book. His second, *The Last Bush Pilots*, captured the coveted Amazon 2013 Top 100 Breakthrough Novels Award. *Code Name: Dodger* is his first novel, a young adult spy adventure series.

He is currently working on two new books, *There I Wuz! Volume III*, and *Jihadi Hijacking*, Mission 3 of the *Code Name: Dodger* series, due November 2015.

A portion of proceeds from Mr. Auxier's books go to the international orphan relief funds, Warmblankets.org and flyingkites.org

Mr. Auxier makes his home in Phoenix, Arizona.

NOW BOARDING: VOLUME III!

MORE...

—Aeronautical
Adventures
—Inflight Emergencies
—Tough Lessons
—Stories behind the
stories
—Guest Stories
—Love, Laughs and
Tears in the Sky
—How Cap'n Aux
Risked All to Land
his First Captain
Seat

PLUS...

—Cap'n Aux answers Your
aviation questions!
—More surprises!

TARGET PUBLICATION DATE: 6/18/16!

Made in United States
Orlando, FL
03 March 2022

15346716R00078